Rimbaud

HARPER & ROW, PUBLISHERS
New York, Evanston, San Francisco, London

Rimbaud

Yves Bonnefoy

translated by Paul Schmidt

Originally published in France under the title RIMBAUD PAR LUI-MEME.
©1961 by Éditions du Seuil.

RIMBAUD. English translation copyright©1973 by Harper & Row, Publishers, Inc. All
rights reserved. Printed in the United States of America. No part of this book may be used
or reproduced in any manner without written permission except in the case of brief
quotations embodied in critical articles and reviews. For information address Harper &
Row, Publishers, Inc., 10 East 53rd Street, New York, N.Y. 10022. Published simultaneously in Canada by Fitzhenry & Whiteside Limited, Toronto.

LIBRARY OF CONGRESS CATALOG CARD NUMBER: 72-83824

STANDARD BOOK NUMBER: 06-136017-1

Contents

Rimbaud

A Mendicant Childhood

I

To understand Rimbaud let us read Rimbaud; let this be our desire: to separate his voice from the many other voices that have mingled with it. There is no point in seeking elsewhere, at a distance, what Rimbaud tells us himself. Few writers have so passionately sought to know themselves, to define themselves, to transform themselves, to become another man through self-knowledge: let us take this search seriously, for nothing is more serious. I propose to rediscover a voice, to decipher its will, above all to reawaken its tone: this fever, this inimitable purity, these moments of triumph, these falterings.

Let us listen to his voice. And to begin, to perceive its abrupt charm, and also to gauge a certain silence that surrounded it, that attempted to stifle it, and that probably succeeded—let us listen to its bitterest sarcasms, which are the expression, certainly, of its greatest animosities: *my hometown takes first prize for stupidity over all small towns,* declares this sixteen-year-old schoolboy to his teacher. *What a shit-hole!* he will exclaim three years later. *And what monsters of innocence, these peasants . . . I'm at my wit's end. Not a book, not a bar anywhere near here; nothing goes on in the streets! What a horror the French countryside is!* We can follow these litanies of counter-adoration throughout Rimbaud's entire work. There seem to be no words insulting enough to express the horror of this *Arduan cosmorama,* of provincial life: as if it were a kind of remote, inert—and nameless—divinity. Why such anger, which resembles a fascination? But let me recall to those who have known *the country, where you are raised on starchy food and mud* and *that godawful Charlestown* or any other such town, the violent contradictions of life in provincial cities and villages. On the one hand, solitude and the soil, the presence of the elements and their silent duration, a world of real things that can sustain a man of few words *(I am sent back to the soil, to seek some obligation,* Rimbaud will write one day, *to wrap gnarled reality in my arms. A peasant!);* on the other, the veil that has fallen across this original plenitude, a rigid social life without any horizon, an impoverished speech that vitiates true silence, the dogmatism of narrow communities where, as everybody watches everybody else (that Arthur Rimbaud for instance, who wears his hair long and smokes his pipe with the bowl pointing down), the spirit quickly erodes. Slow-paced walks in the late afternoon, stifling the soul in revolt—Rimbaud suffered from them enough to set them up in his poems, making their eternities eternal:

> *On Railroad Square, laid out in little spots of lawn,*
> *Where all is always order, the flowers and the trees,*
> *All the puffing bourgeois, strangling in the heat,*
> *Parade their envious nonsense on Thursday afternoon.*

Railroad Square, *laid out in little spots of lawn . . .* There is a tortured resentment in this poem *(A la musique)* that is the origin of a struggle. There was, in 1870, a very young Rimbaud, timid, *in messy clothes,* obsessed by a thousand desires, who wandered despairingly through these hopeless, loveless streets. He could not bear that perennial boredom, nor that the future, the possible, had disappeared there, in front of that railroad station which opened only onto other identical stations, beneath a clock measuring useless time. He would not be reduced, like his little sister Vitalie, to counting trees for lack of a life to lead. "One hundred and eleven chestnut trees on the Mall, sixty-three near the station," notes in her diary Vitalie, who was soon to die.

Provincial towns are bad educators because they destroy freedom. Provincial towns are the "negative" absolute. But now, in this word, I want to point out not only a supreme peril, but a kind of chance, for the absolute engenders the absolute, and the deepest alienation is that which can lead, if a barrier falls, to the most violent poetry. It is because of Rimbaud that we can define—and stress the value of—those sudden reconversions of the self, those new beginnings, that brutally reveal, rocking and swaying before us, in a pure, wild moment, the city halls and the post offices—all those places of daily life that are the more pernicious when habit prevents us from seeing them. At such moments, the very absence of any existential escape opens, through these appearances suddenly stripped of their usual meaning, through the strangeness of the Useful, now paralyzed, the way to a new, and radically different, possibility, to a new relationship between man and being. I will say more about this poetic experience, the beginning of a transmutation described in *Alchimie du verbe*. It may be that the barren face of small-town dereliction is a favorable condition for perceiving the most essential freedom.

For the moment, to finish settling Rimbaud in the loneliness of his first years, let me recall another form of extreme rejection of French provinciality, one which declared itself in 1789. There was also in the Revolution, perhaps above all else, a radical challenge to all existing customs, a metaphysical quality of violence, which may be considered the political expression of an existential suffocation. Rimbaud stands not far away from Ruhl, the member of the Convention who, in the main square of Reims, smashed the Sainte-Ampoule, the vessel of inexhaustible oil used to consecrate the kings. Ruhl killed himself less than a year later. *I have never been one of you,* Rimbaud was to write in *Une Saison en enfer; I have never been a Christian; I belong to the race that sang on the scaffold; I do not understand your laws; I have no moral sense; I am a brute* . . . Rimbaud belongs to the race of those metaphysical rebels who haunt the peaceful countryside, an *inferior race,* yes, if it is true that it cannot adapt, cannot possess, cannot prosper, that it tends only toward death. But he understands, and by that decides his fate, that it is a holy race: *Still a child, I admired the hardened convict on whom the prison door will always close; I used to visit the bars and rented rooms his presence had consecrated . . . I followed his fatal scent through city streets.* And he himself was to be poetry's convict, one, I mean, whom a need to deny the deadening provincialisms in Western culture impels—and in *Matinée d'ivresse* he says it as clearly as Nietzsche—beyond good and evil.

II

But the fact is that he also bore, and with more suffering than any other, the burden of good and evil. When he was *still a child,* Rimbaud lived not only in this Christian Europe he was to denounce with such passion and to leave; he also lived in one of its most sterile, puritanical recesses, the despotic empire of Mme Rimbaud, his mother. Much has been written about Vitalie Cuif, and it is not agreeable to scrutinize matters of family life, even in the name of poetry, but how, if we are fully to understand Rimbaud's earliest voice, can we avoid seeing him between *Charlestown* and *la mother,* those paired powers that he once named in English to charm away their peril? On one hand, the inescapable horizon of the Ardennes. Rimbaud was born in 1854, in Charleville, in a family of landed proprietors whose well-dowered daughter had married a career officer. And the whole of his childhood passed between the successive maternal establishments—on the main street or another "sous les Allées"—and two schools, the Institution Rossat, where he enrolled late, and the Collège on the lonely Square of the Holy Sepulchre. Yet even on those streets and in those classrooms, he seemed —and also his brother Frédéric, a year older than he—mysteriously isolated. "Usually," wrote their friend Ernest Delahaye in his *Souvenirs familiers,* "schoolboys laugh and shout a lot when they play; but these two barely exchanged a few brief words, and they seemed to prefer silence to accompany their games." The brothers seemed to belong to another, harsher realm of moral constraints. For a long time they used to be taken by their mother to market with their two sisters, in procession, as if it were necessary to emphasize their difference and their loneliness. First, noted Louis Pierquin, there came "the two little girls, Vitalie and Isabelle, holding hands; in the next line came the two boys, also holding hands; Mme Rimbaud brought up the parade at the prescribed distance." This little army bobbed its way over the round paving stones of the great Place Ducale, among baskets of eggs and crates of vegetables; passers-by were surprised at such severity, and such folly.

Mme Rimbaud seemed bent on cultivating loneliness around her child. She had soon separated from her husband. She had never lived with him, to be more precise, except during the brief periods between Captain Rimbaud's garrison assignments. Her husband was lively and adventurous; indolent one minute and violent the next, his younger daughter Isabelle wrote later, but perhaps she invented it. He might have been able to provide his son with some outlet for his mind, but he as well could not endure his wife's ungraciousness, and quickly developed the habit of living apart from her. He stopped seeing her for good in 1860, probably when his last child was born. Let us note that he did not die until 1878, in Dijon, about the time his son was beginning a second existence in Alexandria and Cyprus. But they never saw one another again, and there was nothing between them but that pewter dish, thrown violently to the floor by the husband and again immediately afterwards by the wife in an early quarrel which, wrote Ernest Delahaye, resounded "forever" in Rimbaud's memory.

With Rimbaud there was Frédéric, the oldest, lazy and commonplace, of no help, and two cowed little sisters, Vitalie and Isabelle. Nothing that could attenuate the incessant confrontation, openly or covertly violent, in which he had been trapped by his mother's anxiety and resentment.

It is generally agreed that she was very harsh. And let us not underestimate the brutality of a woman capable, according to eye-witnesses, of taking a broom to chase her own granddaughters from her door step; they were guilty of bearing her son 'Frédéric's blood; he had made a "bad" marriage that she eventually managed to break up anyway. "The two of you have ruined my life," Frédéric said on his deathbed to the drab, possessive Isabelle.

We cannot help but think of Rimbaud's words: *You, parents, have ruined my life, and your own!* Mme Rimbaud was a creature of obstinacy and hidden hatreds, avaricious, proud and unfeeling. She was a figure of pure energy, borne along by a faith that verged on bigotry, and besides, if we are to believe her extraordinary letters of 1900, in love with extinction, with death. In this brief essay I cannot quote, however much her portrait requires it, those enthusiastic descriptions of burials and exhumations. Let us simply observe that at the age of seventy-five she had the gravediggers lower her into her tomb, between the coffins of Vitalie and Arthur, for a delectable foretaste of darkness.

She was so inhuman, surely, because of some profound disturbance. It was not that she revered social conventions (she tolerated her son's shoulder-length hair when it was the laughing-stock of Charleville; she was to accept Verlaine with astonishing indulgence), but she had decided to live by absolute values in order to contain her neuroses, and not to end like her two brothers : one, "the African," had run away to Algeria at seventeen and died after a burned and wandering life at thirty-one; and the other was able to accept life only through drinking, and he also fled, escaping the sister who had wanted to rule him and was only able to take some of his money; he soon squandered his inheritance and grew old a vagabond.

There was the hurt of her broken marriage as well. *"Madame" in the open field stands too straight,* wrote Rimbaud in *Mémoire,* with clairvoyance and a kind of love, and we can imagine the woman well enough, stubborn yet perhaps in love, still prizing long after her separation the proud rigidity that had caused it. *Regrets for the thick arms, and young, of virgin grass,* adds Rimbaud. He introduces the image of the sheet of water, *this sourceless water, unmoving, grey,* where he, the *motionless rowboat,* remains paralyzed.

She was doubtless attached to the little boy. *The flesh of childhood,* in later prose writings, remains worthy of regret. *Ah! childhood, grass and rain, the puddle on the paving stones, moonlight, when the clock strikes twelve!* But Mme Rimbaud soon came to detest the thought of her son becoming "un bout d'homme" and being taken from her, he as well, by the world and mentality of men. She tried to interrupt this necessary development. She wanted at least to smother any desire for independence, any attempt at freedom. The consequence, in one who thought of himself as an orphan, was a profound ambivalence, a mixture of hatred and fascination. Because he was not loved, Rimbaud obscurely inferred he was guilty, and with all his innocence he turned fiercely against his judge. *Along the rivers the little children sit, stifling their curses . . .* But to be denied in his role as a man impelled him to become one in her presence, ready to love, ready to replace his father, and, soon disappointed by her unyielding coldness, ready for negative attitudes once again. Too soon an adult, and too long the *little child.*

He is like his mother; he has her obstinacy, perhaps her naiveté, certainly her peasant materialism, later on her avidity, and her pride. Is this perhaps the reason he remains so often passive before her, slapped and accepting it, expressionless, though in secret he nourishes the deepest *loathings?* Yet even when vanquished his mind remains free. Rimbaud was always lucid. I think of that admirable poem, *Les Poètes de sept ans.* We can accept it as a true picture of this childhood, and see in it in action the liberating power of the mind.

What was Rimbaud at the age of seven? In that life constructed crisis by crisis, the first one occurred surely at just that age, after the birth of Isabelle, when his parents had already separated. His grandfather, Nicolas Cuif, had just died. Mme Rimbaud left the large apartment on the "Grande Rue" for a more modest place, temporary as a matter of fact, in a working-class house; there she increased her severity, intending to keep her children from contact with the poor children in the neighborhood. "Madame" has a grudge against her husband and the world. She displays for their benefit the gloomy splendor of crêpe de chine and eternal black dresses. Arthur Rimbaud, now beyond his first childhood, weighs his loneliness—but in the workers he watches returning home in the evening, in their very fatigue and their poverty, he also comes upon the idea of transforming the cruel society that forces him to be alone. From the very first his poetry is revolt, as it is love disappointed, as it is a desire for a *new love*.

III

To bring this relation of a childhood to a close, I would like to examine *Les Poètes de sept ans*, to put forth a perspective in which I believe Rimbaud's life and thought can be almost grasped.

For that we must begin by asserting his desire for love, a vocation for love, the *deep tenderness* he wrote about. This feeling will persist throughout his work, in spite of sarcasms and denials, like a trusting disposition, like an appeal. *Loving—either Psyche's peril, or her strength.* The whole of *Les Déserts de l'amour*, especially, bears witness to this expectation. These pages, among the noblest and most moving that Rimbaud wrote, repeat it over and over with the anguish of a bad dream, and a sad awareness that it will be forever vain. For it is also true that Rimbaud never sought love without anticipating its failure. *And finally, when you are hungry or thirsty, there is someone to chase you away*—this is the end of a fantasy, in one of the *Illuminations* whose title, moreover, is *Enfance*. It seems to bear witness to experiences of violence and frustration that have not been forgotten—those, I believe, which were inflicted on him by his mother. She exiled him, through too little love, from the land he could have lived in. I mean from the world of trust, where we dare think, despite the ever present possibility of suffering, that things and beings are not necessarily hostile or illusory. What irreparable destruction can be wrought by a primordial lie! *How good, these blue eyes—but they lie.* Look at Mme Rimbaud : the attentions she pays her child, the watch she keeps over him, the care, perhaps even the excessive care, she takes of him. But this most lucid of children cannot help but perceive in her unimaginative behavior nothing more then an unfeeling sense of duty. It resembles love, it's true, because attention and watching and caring are signs of love. But these are signs that *lie;* pure form, without content. And in place of a world of rich, full relationships, the kind of world love creates when it is freely given, Rimbaud perceives only a soulless mechanism born of obligation. The child experienced the emptiness of signs, and their falseness. A duality appears between their pretensions and their emptiness. They wither, betraying the fact that they are only surfaces, and they cause to wither all that they inhabit, without meaningful content from then on. Things seem to have a soul when love makes a claim upon them. But as soon as they are abandoned by love, they are nothing more to the disappointed eye than opaque, lifeless bodies. Even a mother, whom bonds of affection make transparent to a child, becomes opaque—a mystery, but of the evil kind. And all the daily world as well, everything human, everything man uses for what he claims to be purposes of love—places, dwellings, and objects—will also reveal themselves as enemies and seem ugly, distorted. Out of this abandoned wreckage arise the grotesque, the sordid, and the excremental. For Rimbaud, who had discovered, or thought he had discovered, the great lie of love, these were the proofs he needed. And he will proclaim their presence—in *Les Assis*, in *Accroupissements*—as giving the lie to hypocritical idealization, and as the negative transcendence of man's nonbeing, of his low and vile nature over his pretensions to light. He will be in communion with them, like the anxious dispossessed child in *Les Premières Communions*, who *passed her holy vigil in the outhouse* as a witness to the falseness of communion in love.

Izambard, Rimbaud's rhetoric teacher, in a crucial observation, reports that "each new set-to with his mother caused a flowering of scatological images in his poems." Rimbaud used to call his mother "la bouche d'ombre" (the mouth of darkness). This sense of opaqueness, this obsession he had with the blemishes of existence, are a direct consequence of the delusiveness of his mother's love. And this I consider truly a profound metaphysical aggression that Rimbaud underwent as a child. It forced him into his *atrocious scepticism*, into aggressiveness and anguish. It robbed him of that trusting disposition which is in life the inventive and creative element. Indeed, to understand Rimbaud we must return to the teachings of Platonism; and remember that a metaphysics of love, which assures us that it helps us overcome the instincts, find remission of exile, reach participation in *the true life*, has at least a psychological reality and reflects the force which raises our existence to being. Robbed of love, Rimbaud was deprived of that possible communion with what is. And he saw reality, like his own mind, split into dangerous dualities.

To begin with, in very early childhood, there was the awareness (so liberating in one sense, so "poetic") of another world, more transparent and more free, beyond the confines of this one. The *Illuminations* contain a thousand traces of this childhood fantasy. In *the great house, its windowpanes still streaming* (we are already beyond the real world, the mind is vagabond, opaqueness has dissolved, the inimical sky cleared) we realize that Rimbaud was one of those children *in mourning* who *looked at marvelous picture books*. And such children invent an *elsewhere*. When they see, or think they see, *a little ribbon-covered cart, abandoned in the hedge or rolling away down the path,* or *a troupe of tiny strolling players all dressed up, seen on the road at the edge of the woods;* when the circus stops for a while in town *(Parade of Enchantments. This is how it was: chariots carrying animals of gilded wood, masts and motley tents pulled by twenty spotted circus horses at a great gallop, and children and men, on the most amazing beasts);* when, in magazines, they look at *Spanish and Italian girls who laugh,* they experience a feeling of deliverance, they want to run away from where they live, without understanding, unfortunately for them, that it is that very place they must first transform.

We are not yet born, Rimbaud was to write. *The true life is lacking.* And he quickly found himself facing a deeper opposition. The *here,* the depressing moral horizon, is decidedly the opposite of life in accord with nature, which is in its essence innocent and free, and open to the rays of universal love. Man has fallen from the transparence that was his by birth, says *Soleil et chair.* He has forgotten *the eternal birth of Venus* . . . In Rimbaud, trust in nature is intact; trust in the grass, the flowers, the dawn, in the clouds above the high seas. His well-known thirst is perhaps no more than the transfer to earthly springs still accessible of another, more secret thirst that remains unquenched. And the filth which he finds also in nature does not compromise it for him, as it destroys human pretension; on the contrary, it is proof of the spiritual and moral superiority of nature, which never stoops to the ignoble game of idealization. *Oh! the little fly, drunk at the urinal of a country inn, in love with rotting weeds; a ray of light dissolves him!* Natural light dissolves the signs of opaqueness—without, alas, being able to encompass one who adores its splendor. *I dragged myself through stinking alleys, and with my eyes closed I offered myself to the sun, the god of fire.* Even wrapped in the most luminous rays, Rimbaud's soul remains incurably dark.

I have gathered here feelings and beliefs that Rimbaud has scattered throughout his work.

And we will have to rediscover them with him, following the development of his thoughts until the moment they break off. We will have to recognize their truth, at least to understand them as poetic truth, but I want to remain a moment with that child Rimbaud was, with the trusting man he deserved to become, and I want to show the harm that these ideas caused him by coming to him so early. It may be that we have to think the human condition a lie, our society a failure, our existence half stifled. The truth may well be that we must today oppose our *hysteria* (as the moving and serious voice of *Les Premières Communions* calls it) to *eternal Venus*. But these are adult matters, and the consciousness of our misfortune that the young Rimbaud took generously upon himself, established so precociously in a mind still juvenile, could only aggravate his self-contempt, and since no one can love if he begins by hating himself, could only separate him from simple natural beauty whose worth he nonetheless affirmed. It was his awareness also that destroyed him. He will try by travelling to return to the realm of the marvellous images; by the *systematized disorganization of all the senses* to reawaken the immediacy of nature; but he will always carry with him that self-disgust described in *Honte,* as well as unresolvable contradictions of soul and body.

And, for example : a heart, *delicate mysterious ways,* the kindness attested by the *foolish virgin* in *Une Saison en enfer;* and at the same time the resolute hate, the wickedness that we might call a mask, were it not penetrating so far into his being, destroying him. *I steeled myself against Justice. I fled. O witches, o misery, o hate, my treasure was left in your care! I have withered within me all human hope. With the silent leap of a sullen beast, I have downed and strangled every joy.* Rimbaud would try, in 1873, to exorcise his demon, but in vain. For the most profound of his contradictions, and also the most deadly, is between a weakness and a strength. He is the indefatigable walker, the restless discoverer; in Africa he will be a dogged worker, full of an energy set free—as in a saint, or the *hardened convict*—by an inaptitude for other human endeavors. Yet when it comes to the problem he is trying to solve, he will also be deprived of all resource, *robbed.* He is well aware of it, in any case; also that he is the *slave* of his baptism. He knows quite well that beyond provinciality or mother, there is still another enemy, triumphant, Christianity. *Christ! Oh Christ, eternal thief of energies!* In *Les Premières Communions* (and also, but much later, in *Une Saison en enfer,* in the *Illuminations)* religion is presented less as a distortion of the mind than as an exhaustion of the entire being. And this may perhaps explain that last of Rimbaud's contradictions, so strange at first glance, between the pure intellectuality of his search and the material means, alcohol and drugs, he accepts to attain its goals. Just as emotional estrangement has become a *poison,* almost a physical sickness, so Rimbaud has to reawaken a disconcerted animal energy in order to recover the *state of child of the Sun.* When the mind alone is at work, Rimbaud knows himself beaten before he has begun.

Rimbaud, so injustly dispossessed. But in the crucible of his lack, let us also recognize the unforseen gold that estrangement and adversity can provide; and, going further, let us suggest another determinism, and consequently another form of criticism, than those that sociology or psychology propose. If Rimbaud, in fact, has become Rimbaud, if we are entitled to contrast his banal condition with such resolute poetry, then beyond Marxist or Freudian analyses, for example, we have to find another necessity that might specifically elucidate this transmutation of victim into poet. Such a necessity is metaphysical. It deals not with the nature of things, but with their being. And it all seems, in fact, as if the very degradation of being, the degradation of the possible into something inert and objectified (society, moralizing religion, closed morality, dead things) had to be faced and assumed voluntarily, totally, brutally, by someone set apart precisely in order to make possible that *awakening* that poetry attempts. Then, in this place of ashes, where, always, a spark subsists (a memory, a distant reminiscence, *Man of average constitution, was the flesh not once a fruit, hanging in an orchard? Oh infant hours! Was the body not a treasure to be unsparing of? Loving—either psyche's peril, or her strength?*), the fire revives. And there was in fact, just before the turn of the century, a universal crisis of love. "We have destroyed love of life in our strange hearts," wrote Villiers de l'Isle-Adam, "and have been reduced to our souls in this very existence! To agree to live, from now on, would only be sacrilege toward ourselves." This is more or less what Mallarmé thought, and an entire literature was to arise from this yielding to the fatalities of the era—but Rimbaud alone was to try to *reinvent love,* to become the *thief of fire,* placing himself thus within what I would like to call the heroic causality . . . Yes, two responses can be made to any historical situation. Either "understand" it, for conservation or change (and certainly this acceptation will be more successfully described by psychological or social analyses, those which have causality for their principle), or revolt against it, try to give life to the existential virtualities that it stifles—and this marks at the same instant the limits of causal analyses and the beginning of poetry. For consciously attempting the impossible is at least, in the fixed and dark world of necessity, a reawakened awareness of being, an illuminating intuition like that of death.

True poetry, that which is a new beginning, that which helps revive, is born in the very presence of death. What we call a "poetic vocation" is simply a will to resist, eventually in most cases made vain by ordinary existence, which is a leaden sleep, a sleep that leads to death.

Darkness and Light

I

Love has to be reinvented—this, then, was Rimbaud's task. And to accomplish it, to return the real to its primordial transparence, to find access again to *the true life*, it is natural enough that he should have turned to language. For words, when man is lost in darkness, have a singular capacity for giving light. Even if the thing they name has been compromised by daily life, words seem to preserve a purer essence. Named, the thing is revealed in its primitive splendor. Said, if only we pronounce the word gravely, without any practical intent, it seems ready to receive us into another world, where nothing would separate the most earthly existence from *the streaming purity of boundless life*. Poetic language suggests being—whence comes the hope it gives us. But that hope we have to challenge immediately. For to love words, to enter that luminous realm—is this not in fact to lose what we seek and to grasp at its shadow? We will have enjoyed the pleasures of fantasy, yet reality (the *gnarled reality* that Rimbaud will never forget) will all the more escape us. Poetry may be beautiful, nor does it lack virtues, at least at the dawn of our desire. But it is a queen without a realm, destined to penury when evening comes. *I want her to be queen!*

writes Rimbaud in the *Illuminations*. And he goes on to describe almost without bitterness this moving and illusory couple, man and his fantasy: *And indeed, they were royal; all morning long, when scarlet draperies hung upon the houses, and in the afternoon, when they appeared at the edge of the gardens of palms.*

Poetic expression, therefore, is both a hope and a threat. But as a consequence it may at least constitute a state of watchfulness, and allow us to escape from the greatest of the misfortunes of a debased existence, language blinded by everyday use. The believer in poetry is perhaps—by his very involvement in words—more an exile than ever, but emotionally, intellectually, he is kept from losing his soul. *I'm intact,* Rimbaud says in one of the first pages of *Une Saison en enfer.* Poetry may be arid, like solitude, but it often possesses the same invigorating power. A struggle against the debased use of words, it resembles silence, and in Rimbaud's case it is of the exact same nature as his well-known taciturnity, and a forerunner as that was of his final great refusal.

We have a sure indication that Rimbaud was very early aware of the hope that words can give, the transparence they can recreate, the salvation they make us believe in. A Latin poem from his school days, *Ver erat . . .* , has been preserved. Its theme is taken from a short passage from Horace about the doves who crowned him as a child with branches of laurel and myrtle *non sine Dis,* "not without divine intervention"; but Rimbaud's conception goes far beyond this allegory, to the hidden heart of poetry. It is indeed a return to the original transparence, both light and warmth, that his metaphor of the shining fountain asks of poetry, and we can thus understand how Rimbaud will try one day to go searching for his *primitive state of child of the Sun:*

> *A light gleaming with brightness*
> *Poured round my shoulders, wrapping my body in its rays:*
> *Nor was this light at all like the dim light*
> *Mixed with darkness that hangs before our eyes.*
>
> . . .

You will be a poet! and through all my veins, then,
Heavenly warmth flowed, just as a fountain,
Pure shining crystal, flames in the light of the sun.

II

Arthur Rimbaud surely wrote many poems during his school years that are lost today.

Indeed, in the earliest of those that we have, *Les Etrennes des orphelins*, we find a prosodic ease that indicates years of careful work with language. This poem is the last example, and probably the intended masterpiece, of a first manner. As evidence for this forgotten period, more childish than adolescent, it shows that the simplest pleasures of language, naive word harmonies, full rhymes, lively but conventional epithets, bursts of eloquence, were closely associated by Rimbaud with certain humble emotional satisfactions. It is not by accident that the poem is an evocation of little children who *have no mother* and are abandoned throughout the holiday eve; and the lyrical way in which the children are celebrated indicates plainly what compensation is expected from poetic fantasy. The world the poem creates is a little oversweet, pink and blue, the world of sentimental literature where children are always loved. Clearly, Rimbaud asks poetry to assure him the self-esteem he was never taught. Feeling himself motherless, at least he could think that an orphan was an object of universal care.

He looks, in a word, for the ideal, for illusion. And these are ordinary paths, where genius is hardly to be expected. Nor did he, in this beginning of 1870, at fifteen, seem anything of what he was to become. He entered rhetoric class in the fall, still the schoolboy "a bit prim and proper, insipid and well behaved, with clean fingernails, flawless notebooks, astonishingly correct homework, and perfect scholarly class notes" whom Izambard had just met. But early in the year a crisis overtook him. His sensuality broke forth, conferring on the world another order and another meaning, revealing the beauty of bodies as a gold that had remained untouched in the darkness of these dismal surroundings. This was a lesson of hope, for here was a part of reality upon which he could build. And this tool, poetry, this power of words to designate something other than this world, seemed now to have some use. The impatient Rimbaud writes *Sensation* and *Première Soirée*. He opens up language to the life of instinct. The function of poetry is no longer to replace the real, but continually to recall its richness, keeping the senses alert, preparing the mind for the coming conquest of what language could not provide. A *gypsy poetry*, Rimbaud called it. Like the man without social attachments, poetry has to find in *sensations* what is pure nature, freedom's pure ferment. And it also has to formulate a theory of the harmonious life, which *Soleil et chair* does. This poem proclaims its rejection of the estrangements I have described. It "overcomes" them through the dream of *the eternal Venus*, exalting the Panic aspect of life, discovering, beyond maternal betrayal, the generous love of the Earth; and saying in the same breath that *the other God* is evil and we must no longer follow him. *Soleil et chair* is animated by a great strength. In it, we might think that Rimbaud is the master of his fate. And yet how fragile is all this animation without true faith! If there is any strength here, it derives only from the hope, yet untried, that to state a thought, to formulate it, and to endow it with the splendor of poetic expression is a creative process that gives the poet the freedom to conform to it in his own life.

And, it is true, several circumstances had recently strengthened this hope. Just as childhood was coming to an end in Rimbaud, when his mother had somewhat relaxed her harsh, anxious supervision, a very young teacher arrived at the Collège in Charleville, who was a poet, too, and had lived in Paris. Georges Izambard was to be a kind of Providence for his pupil. Not that he was not by nature a timid soul, and too much an "aesthete," opposing poetry to the "bourgeois," which was one of the age's shortcomings and meant nothing, fundamentally, for Rimbaud. But he was enthusiastic and generous, and his friendship and confidence were to hasten the maturity of Rimbaud's intelligence, strengthen his beliefs, harden his decisions. All those months until July when Rimbaud was preparing for his examinations, endlessly composing Latin verses, were also the time of his literary apprenticeship—which he feverishly identified with an apprenticeship for life. The schoolboy found out about the Parnassian movement, the Latin Quarter, publishers, bookstores. *In two years, perhaps in a year*, he wrote to Banville, in a rather artful letter, *I will be in Paris. Anch'io gentlemen of the press, I will be a Parnassian!* And he adds: *You would drive me mad with hope and joy, cher Maître, if you were to have them make a little place among the Parnassians for my piece* Credo in Unam . . . *I could get into the last issue of* Le Parnasse: *it would be a Credo for poets! . . . Ambition! Oh, what madness! . . .*

Banville never published *Credo in Unam* (that is, *Soleil et chair*), and Rimbaud must quickly have become aware of its essential fragility, and learned not to rely on the hope it had expressed. For in those spring months he begins to write satirical poems, and their tone is very different. I think of *Vénus Anadyomène* and *Le Châtiment de Tartufe.* Language here is forced to name the sordid aspects of the world. The first of these two sonnets opposes to the Cypris of *Soleil et chair* a deformed Venus, rising out of a tub in a public bath, *horribly beautiful! . . . she bends and shows the ulcer on her anus.* That summer (*my summer despairs*, Rimbaud was to write much later, and again: *I hate summer; it destroys me*), other poems exacerbate this darkening vision. As early as *Les Réparties de Nina*, stupidity and indifference are discovered in the midst of that sensual beauty that only lately had been for him so rich in hope. Rimbaud may well have had a bad experience with some listless *Nina.* Furthermore, he was soon alone—Izambard had left on vacation —and sickened by the foolishness that was rampant in the national disaster. *It's awful, all these retired grocers dressing up in uniform*, he wrote to Izambard on the twenty-fifth of August, . . . *I'm like a fish out of water here, sick, mad, stupid, and worn out.* But above all else, his doubt grew the more he tried to deny it. *Soleil et chair* was an act of faith. It says quite precisely that love is *the only faith*, and thus implies (which is quite true) that we must believe in love in order for it to exist.

The enthusiasm which had been born with writing having slackened, however, *the horrors and loathings* thrive again.

And so, in a sense, this early poetry written in the spring and summer of 1870 is really creative, though perhaps it did not create, as Rimbaud had wanted, a having, a possession. It created a knowing, since it discovered, despite Rimbaud, that it is not enough merely to speak in order to transform, nor to state in order to be, and that words are no more able to help us to reality when they pretend to than they are to replace it when we have decided to shun it. It discovered that if we wish to change that which is, and to begin with, ourselves, then we must rely on something other than words. We must rely on some component of the actual world. Looked at in this way, Rimbaud's sarcastic or sinister poetry (*A la musique* for example, or *Le Châtiment de Tartufe*) is closer to a revolutionary choice than the exalted turbulence of his great cosmic poem. And *Vénus Anadyomène* is secretly related to that earlier diatribe, *Le Forgeron*. For a long time, if we can believe Delahaye—from the age of thirteen or fourteen—Rimbaud had dreamed of the violent destruction of the society he lived in. And as the year 1870 passed, there formed more clearly in his mind the idea of a new Revolution that would lead to the metamorphosis of the social horizon. The times seemed ripe for it. The very day the school prizes were awarded, when he was covered with all imaginable laurels, a schoolboy for the last time, news came of the first of the Empire's disasters, the defeat of Wissembourg. The established order was beginning to come apart. Was this not because it was made up only of appearances, insufficiently in control of the more real forces (labor, instincts, etc.) whose future alliance would be able to conquer Christianity and return man to love? *We felt within our hearts something like love,* says the revolutionary blacksmith to Louis XVI as he shows him the violent, dirty mob. Workers, the weak, exiles of all kinds—these are Rimbaud's allies. But his own goal is far beyond all social renewal. He is after the reestablishment of the primordial glory, and he will forget politics the moment a more radical means of transmutation seems at hand.

And so, when he ran away to Paris suddenly one evening late in August, leaving his mother and sisters on their walk, and taking the train first to Charleroi, then doubling back toward the capital,[1] we can hardly say whether he yielded to a fatality of action or to the fatality of poetry. There was certainly a revolutionary hunger in his flight. He wanted to be present at the imminent fall of the Empire. Yet he also wanted, in its true place—that mythical Paris of literature—and at the truest moment, to put disappointing poetry to the most decisive proof.

III

But that proof was never put, for he had travelled the last stretch of his trip without a ticket, and got put in prison for it. And, more profoundly, because a reprieve for a moment calmed his anxious mind. He had probably heard Izambard speak of the four Gindre sisters, of their house. And it may be that a desire to get there added a few pointed proposals to the appeals of *Justice* and *the Muse*. In any case, shut up in Mazas prison, Rimbaud sent Izambard a lost child's plea. *I depend on you*, he wrote, . . . *Do everything! I love you like a brother, I will love you like a father . . . And if you get me freed, take me to Douai with you.* Soon delivered, as it happened, he arrived at Izambard's. We must note here that Izambard's mother had died shortly after his birth and that his father, like the father of the children in Rimbaud's poem, was *far away*. But he had been taken in and brought up by the four sisters mentioned above. And he loved them without reservation. *You certainly are lucky you're not living in Charleville anymore!* Rimbaud wrote to him a few days before running away.

Rimbaud in Douai seemed at ease, perhaps even happy. He and Izambard signed up to drill with the National Guard, a small defense assignment with brooms instead of guns (back in Charleville, and with some justice, he would have called it *patrolotism*), and if here he made

1. The Prussians had cut the direct line from Rethel to Reims on August 29th. Rimbaud's departure may have been hastened by his fear of being kept by the war from going to Paris for a long time.

no objection to drilling on the town field nor to a retired sergeant-major, there is no doubt that it was because of the indulgence and good humor of the first emotional tranquillity he had ever experienced. Those were unforgettable days, away from his mother. Izambard was forced at last to take him back to Charleville, and this only friend had hardly left before Rimbaud ran away again, on October 7, following the beautiful roads that led toward Belgium, and toward Douai. By the tenth he was already back at the Gindre sisters' house. Izambard, who at the call of *the mouth of darkness,* had been vainly following his traces to Fumay, to Charleroi, to Brussels, finally found him in Douai, quietly copying "for the printer" onto brand-new pages the poems he had written on the road.

The notebook, luckily, has been preserved. And it proves that it was on the roads of the Ardennes, in a rush of hope, that Arthur Rimbaud wrote his most limpid poems, his most joyously free, most freely child-like poems. On the road to Charleroi, between fir trees and streams, in the October light, the skies cleared for a moment. That fabulous *elsewhere* where all problems disappear had not yet been encountered, but *here* at least, the sinister *here,* had been left behind, and the very hardships of the road, the hunger and the cold at night, seemed a small price to pay for a real beginning. The walker leaves behind the opaqueness of reality. The changing physical horizon seems a promise of salvation. Everything seems possible; and poetry is reborn with this possibility and becomes one with it. Words speak of the purity and light of another world, as they always do, and now the things along the road, only glimpsed, never belying the words, the *half-cold drinks,* the *inns,* the *servant girls,* appear to be the secret signs of some miraculous welcome yet to come. *Dreamy Hop o' my Thumb, I made up rhymes as I ran* . . . The little boy whose parents wanted to get rid of him, but whose own energy was enough to regain the power to move ahead and the courage to hope, does he near his true habitation, the *château* that towers beyond the imperfect *seasons?* Never again, even in *Matinée d'ivresse,* where something harsh and wounded yet remains and where the soul is still shadowed, will Rimbaud give the impression he gives in these few poems—*Au Cabaret vert, La Maline, Ma bohème*—that he thinks he has reached the gates of *the true life.*

But he stopped, and the illusion was over. At Douai, a few days later, nothing new: only an order from his mother to have him sent home "free of charge" under police escort. *But no one leaves.* There is no *refuge,* no *château,* and *to go on walking can lead only to the end of the world.* Yes, Rimbaud was thinking of this too clearly decisive test when he wrote, in *Une Saison en enfer,* his bitterest lines: *Ah! My life as a child, the open road in every weather; I was unnaturally abstinent, more detached than the best of beggars, proud to have no country, no friends— what stupidity that was!—and only now I realize it!* Redoubled obsessions began to darken his poems.

On those Belgian roads and in Douai—in *La Maline* or *Au Cabaret vert,* but as well in *Les Effarés*—he had found things as he wanted them to be, innocent, transparent. He had begun during those happy days to know himself, to clear himself, to cure himself, and I have no doubt— as Izambard in fact assures us—that *Les Poètes de sept ans* was at least sketched out during this period. For if it is true that there is real intellectual and literary progress between the sonnets written on the road and this great poem of self-knowledge, it is also true that Rimbaud developed very quickly during this period, and above all it is only then that he possessed such objectivity, such serenity, such perspective. Brought back to his mother's, and probably welcomed as before with what Izambard called "a monstrous thrashing," Rimbaud wrote his teacher on November 2: *I am dying, rotting in platitudes, nastiness and greyness;* and for a long time after that he was to be the slave of a repetitive poetry, heavy with all the ashes of his hates and fears.

I think of *Les Assis,* of *Oraison du soir,* of *Chant de guerre parisien,* of *Mes petites amoureuses,* of *Accroupissements,* of *Les Pauvres à l'église,* all poems from the following months. Writing, once an exaltation, has now only the cathartic function of anger. What I have been trying to define with the word "opaqueness," the sarcasm of things, the cynical insinuations of ugliness, the preponderance of things gross and rank upon the soul, has this time almost conquered. It was an unstable and somber period, that winter and spring of 1870–71. Aimless wandering in the country, aimless reading at the public library in Charleville, broken ideas in the squalling winds of the winter landscape. So violent was Rimbaud's revolt that he refused to go back to school. On the first of January he had watched a Prussian bombardment destroy Mezières, next door to Charleville; along the roads he had seen the houses and the little châteaus that the war had boarded up, and he loved these metaphors of a more essential absence. *You follow the red road to come to the empty inn. The château is for sale; its shutters hang loose. The priest has probably gone away with the key to the church. The keepers' lodges all about the park are uninhabited. The fence is so high you can see only the rattling tree-tops beyond* . . . Boundless countryside: a source of strength despite everything during this worst period of exile. When we read *Les Assis*, the savage poem of a persecutor persecuted, haunted by the absolute, we verify that in this vision obsessed by human decay the light of nature, clouded, yet remains intact. Does not Rimbaud discover, in the degraded old chairs, and does he not honor, in their broken caning, *the soul of suns gone by?* His brutal, dangerous expressionism is illuminated and healed by this pure gleam of light.

I can imagine this world of tempests and sudden clearings about him and within him. The world, later, of *Michel et Christine* or of *Larme*, when, *toward evening, the sky filled with storms;* a world of sliding sheets of dark water, of bursting thunderclouds, but also of sudden streaks of red. *When I was a child, my vision was refined in certain skies,* Rimbaud was to write later on. The incessant Baudelairean question, "Can one illuminate a dark and muddy sky?" was in his heart, and if we think of the poem of *Les Fleurs du mal* "L'Irréparable" and its so meaningful inn, which perhaps led Rimbaud to a similar symbolism (I have just referred to *the empty inn*), we can understand at its genesis, both physical and metaphysical, what it is that Rimbaud will later call an *Illumination*. We know that Rimbaud first gave the word the English meaning *painted plates,* and that it probably involved a memory of the *marvellous picture-books* where as a child he sought to forget the place where he was born. And the word contains not so much the notion of sudden knowledge, of intellectual gnosis, of a spiritual vision, than the break-through of hope, the shining-forth of grace, in a fleeting instant. Therefore, however darkened and murky it may be, his world is a magic world, since all good there is expected from a metamorphosis. The least thing there may turn out to be a key, and may inspire the sacred terror that flares up when the supernatural is at hand. *A vaudeville's title filled me with awe,* we read in *Alchimie du verbe,* and I imagine that one of these titles had been "Michel et Christine" and thus alluded to Scribe's vaudeville, in which a young woman who keeps an inn has loved a timid boy—supreme happiness made suddenly conceivable through the very awkwardness of Scribe's work, an awkwardness which has the color of the absolute.

What I liked, Rimbaud says (also in *Alchimie du verbe*), *were: absurd paintings, pictures over doorways, stage sets, circus back-drops, shopsigns, twopenny prints; old-fashioned literature, church Latin, erotic books full of misspellings, the novels our grandmothers read, fairy-tales, little children's books, old operas, silly old songs, naive rhythms of country rimes.* We find here whatever does not represent, but suggests, whatever is simple enough to be used to imagine an *elsewhere.* All "naive" art is an art of initiation. *I used to believe,* adds Rimbaud, *in every kind of magic.*

And I think I am right in saying that during that winter and spring Rimbaud did not so much give in to the darkness of things (despite *Les Assis,* despite *Accroupissements*) as radicalize his hope, making it deeper and more absolute. He brought it from one impossibility after another in this world, to a state of expectation of some kind of grace. Without realizing it, he had laid the basis for a decisive conversion that I will have to talk of soon. Yet, at the moment, he was in very great danger. He could not forget that writing had proved a failure. Without trying to read too much into Delahaye's testimony (he "took pleasure in ascribing to himself the most horrifying and contemptible professions, as well as habits whose description, which he documented ferociously, were enough to bring all the fires of heaven down upon the windows of the café"), we may be sure that homosexuality, never completely accepted, added now to his distress. Moreover, the third time he had run away, from the February 28 to March 10, his first real stay in Paris, had been nothing but disillusionment and wretchedness. He hadn't met the poets, he had hung around in the streets and slept on the banks of the Seine, and had finally started back to Charleville on foot. *Ah! Those stinking rags, bread soaked with rain, drunkenness, and the thousands of loves that nailed me to the cross! . . . I can see myself again, my skin corroded by dirt and disease, hair and armpits crawling with worms, and worms still larger crawling in my heart, lying among ageless, heartless strangers . . . I could easily have died there.* Finally, there was the danger of the approaching summer, the season of unmoving light, and its despair.

Rimbaud on the roads of the Ardennes, crossing the nearby Belgian frontier[2] with Delahaye, hating the customs man's ambiguous searching hands, is certainly no longer *the wanderer,* full of such pure hope, of the fall of 1870. Should he not accept the death that everything suggested to him, death of the mind, death of the soul, the profound death of freedom? But freedom dies only when we accept its death. Like hope, the smaller it becomes in our existence, the more radical it may be if we wish it, and the more capable of an absolute act. Such, precisely, was Rimbaud's will. No matter what respite he might have gained, he never agreed to sell his soul. *I persist stubbornly,* he wrote to Izambard after his second return home, *in worshipping free freedom.* The reduplication has a good deal of meaning. How better to express the idea of the most essential freedom, its attraction beyond all motives? Rimbaud knows himself and expresses himself with genius now, which should not surprise us. For genius, at least where poetry is concerned, consists precisely in being faithful to freedom.

2. At that time, French inhabitants of the border used to go to Belgium for less expensive tobacco.

The Decision

I

And during the month of May, always the time of his greatest
energy in his decisions and in his writing, he got a sudden hold
on himself, he faced the danger that was pressing hard upon him, and
seemed for a moment to escape from it. This is the confrontation that
the *Lettre du voyant* describes, and it is an exemplary action. For in it
freedom at its barest, deprived of any tangible expectation, reveals its
own richness, its creative power, literally its poetry.

What danger threatened Rimbaud most? Self-disgust, obviously. *I
spend my life sitting,* he writes, *like an angel in a barber's chair.* And
in a letter to Izambard, *I am getting myself cynically kept. I dig up old
idiots from school: the stupidest, dirtiest, nastiest things I can think of
I dish up for them . . .* He was unable to conquer a baleful fatality, he
had become the obsessed author of *Accroupissements,* the frightened
disparager of *Mes petites amoureuses,* and so he concludes, coura-
geously, that he himself is ignoble. *I am well aware that I have always
been of an inferior race.* I belong to the race of the conquered and the
enslaved, he believed. Perhaps as well he saw with anguish the Commune's disastrous end; it so resembled him, a revolt of the deprived,

begun during the disorders of the war, continued painfully, hopelessly, by men without illusion. Rimbaud did not go to Paris during the fighting, although some critics long tried to believe the opposite. His letters of May 13 and 15, 1871, seem to prove that he never left Charleville. But the lines of *Les Mains de Jeanne-Marie* or of *Paris se repeuple* are enough to prove that his heart was with the *dark and nameless* in the city in revolt. It was a struggle he understood. He envisioned himself near the burning palaces, less an actor than a witness, aware of its inner meaning: *Good luck, I cried, and I saw a sea of flames and smoke rise to heaven, and left and right all wealth exploded like a billion thunderbolts.*

Yes, it was at the beginning of May, with the waning of the Commune, that he experienced what was almost despair. Of all his poems, *Le Coeur volé* (and *Honte*, later, it is true) is the most hazardous and the darkest. The metaphor of a heart spit upon and *spattered with slop* here represents the suffering so long endured by being bereft of love. Added to that is now the idea of total impotence: *How will I act, my stolen heart?* Rimbaud's only recourse, some confidence in poetry, seems to vanish in this line. Had he not experienced, in fact, feelings for poetry that were often mixed, hate and love at the same time? Had the idea that it was not perfectly pure and efficacious not lead him already, with a kind of miserable shame, to make fun of it in Douai, reciting ten times a day to Izambard Montaigne's equivocal words: "The poet perched on the Muses' tripod, pours out wildly whatever happens to be in his mouth . . ." These unpleasant insinuations scarcely differ from the derision of his new poem. They denounce the illusion of an art which pretends to substitute beauty for misery, reality for absence, while it is nothing in fact but nauseous outpourings. *Un Coeur sous une soutane* was surely written about this time. Under a title of similar inspiration, this story speaks of almost the same problem; it shows us an aspect of Rimbaud in the grotesque seminarian, and woman in the form of a silly, ugly girl; and it makes fun of poetry for being no more than detestable ambiguities about ill-smelling shoes that will forever survive the strains of "the lyre" and the illusions of hope.

That does not mean nothing, wrote Rimbaud to Izambard on the thirteenth of May, referring to *Le Coeur volé.* His biographers have therefore attempted to explain the poem in terms of anecdote and supposed occasions of debauchery or drunkenness, but what *Le Coeur volé* profoundly *means,* what it speaks of, is the self-disgust that for a moment came close to submerging Rimbaud's entire being. A nausea from the heart, that would have isolated him from all his former ambition, from any endeavor, any ideal. A terrible state whose outcome could only be paradox, or death.

Rimbaud chose paradox. On the thirteenth and fifteenth of May two letters, resolute, feverish, authoritative, conveyed to Izambard and to Demeny,[1] who were hardly likely to understand them, the philosophy of the *Voyant* (visionary).

II

Perhaps it might be well, in order better to understand a decision that was to reveal itself so purely metaphysical, to pay attention now to another aspect of Rimbaud's childhood, also of great importance: books read and influences undergone. Yet I can only do so incompletely here; and, leaving aside the catechism and the Gospel, crucial interventions of Christ's religion, as fascinating as it was detested, I think it is enough to evoke two or three encounters which are certain and which were essential. Many others have been supposed; but they are hardly more than fantasies. The breadth and the consistency of Arthur Rimbaud's reading have often been much exaggerated.

Of these few encounters the earliest and the one destined to remain the most important was with the writings of Baudelaire. Rimbaud surely knew him by 1871—in the 1868 edition with Gautier's preface—since we can find in *Paris se repeuple, Le Mal, Les Soeurs de charité,* even in *Les Mains de Jeanne-Marie,* the first signs of the influence of the poems of *Les Fleurs du mal.* It was, in fact, principally "Benediction" or "Le Reniement de saint Pierre" that influenced Rimbaud's rhythms

1. A friend of Izambard, whom Rimbaud had met in Douai.

or images. And how could he remain unmoved at the cry of those admirable lines by Baudelaire which recount the curse uttered by the poet's mother, the poet's will to survive, the misery he experienced with women, and at last, the transparent plenitude acquired through suffering?

> Why did I not bring a nest of vipers forth
> Rather than nourish such derision!
> Accursed be the night of fleeting sport
> When my womb conceived my retribution!
> . . .
>
> Yet in the invisible guard of an Angel
> The Child disowned grew drunk on sunlight
> . . .
>
> For I know suffering is the only nobleness
> That earth and hell can never destroy . . .

Rimbaud must surely have conceived an immediate passion for this magnificent faith; and if he was even then not convinced—he who could not carry forward the impulse of faith—he might hope in any case that Baudelaire was justified, for the dark horizon to be transmuted. All throughout *Les Fleurs du mal* there is an intuition of a metamorphosis of being, of a change from lead to gold, of a renovation of the spirit. Here, in this world "where action is not the sister of dreams," appears the idea of poetry as action, at one and the same time analytic intelligence and mysterious chemistry. And Rimbaud follows Baudelaire in a rapid advance along this path. Let us not doubt that it is because he had read *Les Fleurs du mal* that he was able to write *Les Soeurs de charité* and the admirable last sections of *Les Premières Communions*. Never without Baudelaire could he have so soon acquired so great and so assured a knowledge of the soul, never without him could he have found this small amount of self-confidence which allowed him suddenly to judge without hatred, even with that pity which, despite his pessimistic outlook, has something of the accents of love. These are the first poems where Rimbaud appears poetically adult. In them we perceive what might have been his "victory," passage from the *atrocious scepticism* within him to a stoic serenity. But as yet they can speak only of solitude and exile. Both of them deal with the social situation of woman, who should be the mediatrix between man and reality (*Soleil et chair* hinted at it already), but who can no longer fulfil the role because her soul is *rotten*. Christianity has left all life desolate by ravaging the soul of woman; and woman, from now on the great absence, can provide only a sorrowful warning that Rimbaud hears with a feeling of impotence:

> *Do you know I have destroyed you? Turned your head,*
> *And taken your heart, your life, and your dreams;*
> *I am sick: Oh, lay me down among the Dead*
> *Whose thirst is quenched by dark nocturnal streams!*
>
> *For I was young, and Christ has soured my soul.*
> *He filled me to the throat with sick disgust!*
> *You kissed my hair, my hair as thick as wool,*
> *And I lay and let you . . . Ah, you love your lust,*
>
> *You Men! You little think the woman most in love,*
> *Ruled by a conscience full of sordid terror,*
> *Is prostituted worse than any slave,*
> *And that all our love for you is error!*
>
> *My first Communion is over and past.*
> *I can never have understood your kisses:*
> *For my soul and body embraced by your flesh*
> *Crawled with the rotten kiss of Jesus!*

What a distance between these serious, generous lines and the brutal stanzas of a while previously:

> *Oh my little lovelies,*
> *I hate your guts!*

Go stick fat blisters
On your ugly tits!

Baudelaire has now taught Rimbaud poetic responsibility. And yet what a distance still remains between Rimbaud's *Les Premières Communions* and Baudelaire's "Le Balcon," for example, or any poem where Baudelaire expresses his feelings about love! That difference reveals not so much the hearts, as more or less pure, of these two poets, but their original need. And how much less was the elder deprived!

> Those evenings lit by glowing fires of coal,
> Evenings on balconies, veiled in rosy clouds.
> How sweet I found your breast! How kind your soul!
> We whispered often imperishable words
> Those evenings lit by glowing fires of coal.

There is of course in Baudelaire a good deal of mistrust of woman: he has called her "guilty" and "cold" and even once "abominable." The misery of original sin has marked her much more than man, he thought. But both man and woman, if I may put it this way, are only wounded; they can occasionally sustain each other, contemplate together "the depths of years past," attain poetry at least. There is no absolute separation between them as there is for Rimbaud.

And I believe the following to be true: the transmutation that Baudelaire attempted and the one Rimbaud desired had, without any doubt, the same goal, but for their same alchemy they did not have the same resources, and consequently the younger poet was forced from the path indicated in *Les Fleurs du mal.* Baudelaire wishes to triumph over nothingness. And in a world where being is degraded by man's yielding to fragmentation, self-dilapidation, and death, he realizes that to devote oneself to the limited object, to anything mortal, is the start of a decisive mutation, where the plenitude of existence can be reached with the help of any of its moments. And this devotion is love, which he was luckily given. He had long before been taught, in that "small white house" of his childhood's happy first years, that reciprocated love existed. Rimbaud never received this essential gift. He was thus to try to do without it, or to rediscover it through the act of poetry. But in both cases he came short of that strange happiness, exhausted but ardent, that we sense in the work of Baudelaire. Where the latter, in a word, can call upon "angels clothed in gold" as witnesses because he, like them, has been capable of love, Rimbaud, in spite of himself, knows only the anguish of Lucifer. Before being able to reinvent being he will have to *reinvent love.*

And so, unable to follow Baudelaire where the self can find salvation, he became interested in speculations that suggest more impersonal, more material means for changing lead into gold. There is no doubt that in these months he glanced through certain books on alchemy. But though he was receptive to the alchemic metaphor, he had neither the time nor the inclination to pursue it very far. He says this straightforwardly in *Les Soeurs de charité;* and I think that his interest in both *obscure alchemy* and the *occult sciences* was of the same nature as his taste, attested at this same period, for the librettos of Favart or for oriental tales. An interest, by the way, that was not frivolous for all that, a truly poetic interest indeed, since both Alchemy, the great Art, and Favart's fantastic "dénouements" suggest the same transgression of causality, the same freedom reached through miracles, the same remission and redemption.

More important, however, were other books, as recent research has shown.[2] Brief and scattered reading, as always. We must not exaggerate the importance of Bretagne, an amateur of occult thought whom Rimbaud saw frequently during these last months in Charleville, nor overestimate the latter's patience or even his concern for philosophical theories. All he needed were a few central ideas, a new perspective. In other words, Rimbaud may have read Eliphas Lévi or Ballanche. But even so he never became a student of some system. The ideas he had found in Illuminism or in the Kabala, floating for a while in his thoughts like

2. Cf. Enid Starkie's *Rimbaud.*

distant hopes, came suddenly together only in the attempt, compounded of violence and instinct, to revolutionize his own life.

In any case, here is what occultism and Illuminism suggested to Rimbaud. An ambition, above all, close to his eternal desire—to fix man again within the fabric of being, to return him to the unity that existed at the beginning of time. Also, those ideas—contradictory perhaps, but poetically associable—of the divine: for Eliphas Lévi, a rhythm that man can and must awaken within himself; for Ballanche, a Word temporarily concealed. The world is the word of God, Ballanche teaches, following numbers of others; consequently language, which at one time preserved the substance of things, thanks to the names that Orpheus gave them, remains the key. A poet will come, a hero of the spirit, to reestablish the universal language, and in it and through it, intuitive and all-inflaming, a new reason. Rimbaud could recognize here the mysterious power he had always felt to exist in the poetic use of words. And he also loved the hope spoken of in all the traditions: that man is half-way between God and the darkness of matter; that he bears within him a spark of God; and, as well, that he is free. He is able to determine his salvation.

But to do this, Eliphas Lévi teaches, he must make himself a "voyant" (a visionary), deny the lately come social order, rediscover through an intuition of the divine law, through a kind of brutal and instinctive phenomenology of the sacred, the hidden rhythm of God's things. Ballanche also speaks of a vision, which is reached (for him) through language. Two interests: the core of reality in the one case, language in the other—and here, precisely, in its unceasing contradiction, is the double concern of poetry. Rimbaud, a poet, was acquainted with both poles. Were he to intensify the conflicting quest, would that be enough to attain at last the state of awareness; even to make him the equal of God? At this point the philosophers give him a warning: in any case there is a price to be paid, the worst sufferings, the dismembering of the personality to be accepted; the throwing off of the individual invented by Christianity, who is nothing more than the obscure prison where life now lies, vegetating.

III

And it is at this point as well, probably at the beginning of May 1871, that Rimbaud conceived the extraordinary idea that decided his fate for the next two years, perhaps forever.

That an event occurred at this moment in his existence, a spiritual event, the passion of his two May letters proves amply. He feverishly records there discoveries made in rapid succession, as happens only in a state of crisis. And as for the essential nature of the first intuition, let us not doubt that it was suddenly to have identified the abjection expressed in *Le Coeur volé* with the price asked of the future hero of the spirit: *Right now,* he wrote to Izambard, *I'm depraving myself as much as I can. Why? I want to be a poet, and I am working at making myself a* visionary: *you will not understand at all, and I'm not even sure I can explain it. The problem is to attain the unknown by disorganizing all the senses. The suffering is immense, but you have to be strong, and to have been born a poet. And I have realized that I am a poet . . .* Rimbaud in *Le Coeur volé* expressed the misery of a man both rebelling and scorned. He had seen that his *heart,* his ability to love, had been taken from him, leaving him the prisoner of a fascination for base things, with only the illusory purification that facile, deceitful poetry provides —and with no other recourse, no other act to attempt. And now, skimming *per diletto* through Eliphas Lévi or Ballanche, and reading of the sufferings that have to be undergone in order to become one of the "angels" of the new spirit, but also that *I is someone else,* that one is a receptacle of knowledge without being aware of it, that one can be at the point of revealing that knowledge without being aware of it, he suddenly understands[3] that he is in the process of paying the price, that his unhappiness is the suffering required, and that his very despair is this break-up of the personality, of its finite interests, of its too human

3. I am not trying to invent a "night" like Pascal's for Rimbaud, but simply to emphasize that point in a man's experience when submission to necessity transforms itself into freedom—a central point, often obscure, from which all criticism ought to proceed.

ambitions, that the philosophers were proposing. This exhaustion of will he suffered from so much *(I am getting myself cynically* kept . . .*)* is simply the dissolution of an illusory, in any case degraded, subjectivity: the descent into hell whence he will return a redeemer. Just when he thought himself lost, here he is, by means of an unknown power striving in him, closer than anyone to being a witness to the Spirit. *It's not my doing at all,* he adds. *It's wrong to say: I think. Better to say: I am thought. Pardon the pun.*

Let us understand the pun[4] and what admirable energy this new thought which dresses the wound and cures it has suddenly been able to let loose. The more he had been in despair—and humiliated—the more now his long-frustrated pride proposes him boundless tasks. "I am the One who will create God," Verlaine makes him say later, in "Crimen Amoris." He wants at least to be *the Poet,* that is, *the great invalid, the great criminal, the great accursed—and the Supreme Scientist!* One of those *horrible workers* who, according to Illuminism, are to prepare the return of being, which he was to call *the true life.* This desire *to remake life,* deepening—and so painfully—day after day since childhood, with what metaphysical, eschatological meaning does he now endow it!

He decides, with a courage which now seems to him quite easy, I have no doubt, to follow his destiny, deepening sufferings and torments still more, yet at the same time giving them a positive value and meaning. This estrangement that caused his suffering yesterday is now his glory . . . *But the problem is,* he wrote to Demeny, *to make the soul into a monster, like the comprachicos.*[5] *Think of a man grafting warts onto his face and growing them there . . . All forms of love, of suffering, of madness; he searches, he exhausts within himself all poisons, and preserves their quintessences. Unspeakable torment, where he will need the greatest faith, a superhuman strength . . .* The *horrible worker* can take

4. *C'est faux de dire: Je pense. On devrait dire: On me pense. Penser* (to think) and *panser* (to dress a wound) are homonyms.
5. The "comprachicos" (in Victor Hugo's *L'Homme qui rit,* published in 1869) were kidnappers of children. They deformed them into freaks in order to exhibit them.

upon himself all the repudiations that Arthur Rimbaud had once pronounced so unwillingly. He can take upon himself *Mes petites amoureuses* with less hatred, perhaps, but more detachment—and it is not by chance that this seemingly futile poem has a place in the *Lettre du voyant.* Estrangement has proven to be a creative ascesis. *Vice,* one of the ways of rending the veil that covers up truth. More essentially Rimbaud can now reaffirm his dark poems, *Accroupissements,* a *pious hymn,* he writes, or *Le Coeur volé,* those where the sordid is most dangerously aggressive. *I give you this: is it satire, as you would say? Is it poetry?* These poems in any case are the dissolution, the alchemists' "putrefactio", of *subjective* poetry.

IV

I say one must be a visionary, make oneself a visionary! Rimbaud's main decision was to move from what he called *subjective* poetry to *objective* poetry.

Which is not to mention the fact, he wrote to Izambard, *that your subjective poetry will always be horribly wishy-washy.* And to Demeny, on the subject of Musset: *Oh, those insipid* Contes *and* Proverbes! . . . *Musset didn't manage to do anything worth while; there were visions within those lace window curtains; he closed his eyes.* Subjective poetry seems then to be that poetry which is satisfied with idealized figures, "artiste" aestheticism and verbalism; and that sentimental and lyrical poetry, which preserves only the tameable part of the emotions; that poetry, in a word, which shuts man up in his conventional nature without ever making him aware of the obscure layers of what is. And Rimbaud obviously has not forgotten that for a long time he conformed to this subjective poetry. *Les Etrennes des orphelins* and *Soleil et chair* are of this nature, since their dreams of plenitude so easily are part of torpid existences; and *Ma bohème* or *Le Cabaret vert* and all the sonnets written on the open road, since nothing had ever answered their hopes —these illusions; but the most recent poems are subjective poetry as well, the ones Rimbaud is still in the process of writing, *Les Soeurs de charité* and *Les Premières Communions*, which only describe when it is necessary to transform, and *Les Assis, Oraison du soir,* and *Accroupissements,* since disgust and hate, attitudes both, fix man in the psychological framework of the analysis of alienation. All poetry until this moment has been nothing but such a void. From the point of view of the Kabala this corresponds indeed to the lower level where man vegetates, to that individuality which appeared when primordial being was fragmented. And passing beyond this deceptive poetry, Rimbaud thinks now, will be as well the dismantling of our present misfortune. He proclaims *objective* poetry as a return to the divine life, as a passage from feelings and psychological attitudes to participation regained, as an intensification of our perceptions (which provided only a partial perspective, only a particular tuning of the senses when many others are possible) until they are consumed in the substantial fire of the Unknown. Since our life compared with the life of the Greeks is no longer a harmonious existence, akin to divine rhythms, it is precisely in the burning away of what it has become that we must reinvent the real. Being becomes identified with newness, in the most radical, most *monstrous,* most destructive sense of that term; and truth with a nonmediate vision—with the emergence—of that reality that is ahead of us in the Unknown.

Thus did Rimbaud spiritualize his emotional disintegration, his horrible, martyred soul, giving them meaning and value. Vision, historically unforeseeable, is spiritually the metamorphosis of the emotional distress experienced by an adolescent.

And I will try further on to explain what techniques he attempted to devise in order to learn being, as he almost puts it; what new, hitherto unknown link between language and intuition. For the moment, in his desire for Vision, I would like simply to emphasize the enormous energy that was set to work—for profit, if I may use an expression he hated, but in a new sense, a heroic one. For the Unknown that Rimbaud obscurely senses, burning up the categories of his mind, dispels in so doing the darkness that overwhelmed him. And in a frenzy—with his usual lack of restraint—he hurls himself toward this salvation. For a long time he had tried to replace ordinary sights by fantastic glimmerings. The seven-year-old poet, seeking out Vision, *pressed his thumb against his dazzled eyes,* and the taste expressed in *Sensation* and elsewhere for lukewarm drinks, the odor of wet meadows, the stench of alleyways, revealed the most eager attention to whatever betrays in the familiar appearance of things, the workings of something still beyond denomination. *For a long time,* Rimbaud will say in *Une Saison en enfer, I boasted that I was master of all possible landscapes.* And yet nothing was extraordinary enough to foretell the two great poems that he was to write in the course of the summer; nor that he could send to Banville, whom he seemed only a few months before to respect so much, those pages filled with insolence and genius: *Ce qu'on dit au poète à propos de fleurs.*

I consider this one of the most admirable poems Rimbaud ever wrote, and the expression probably of his energy at its purest. Banville, a *subjective* poet if there was one, had sung on and on about flowers. The soothing decor of his placid imagination was filled with lilies, carnations, and amaranths. It was now time for him to learn that such *enema bags of ecstasy* could be rather rudely insulted in Charleville:

> Always this French vegetation abounds,
> Grouchy, coughing, silly, and sick,
> Where the bellies of basset hounds
> Wallow through the growing dark;

and that someone who called himself a poet had dared to oppose the saps, glucoses, and resins of *industrious plants* to their so-called beauty, in the name of usefulness. The argument is, of course, metaphoric. The sap, coming from beyond the form, makes us think of an epiphany of being. The tangible and the nutritive found in what had been simple enjoyment stress the intoxicating strength of the Unknown. And to submerge being in usefulness and lyricism in commerce, has a polemical value in the struggle against sterile, "subjective" beauty. There seems no doubt that Rimbaud wanted to write, ironically and obliquely, a kind of *ars poetica.* The *"On,"* the persona who addresses the poet on the subject of flowers is still the same monstrous tormented being, both familiar and remote, who had spoken in the letter to Demeny, that *I* who is *someone else* and who may well have shown himself for a moment in the sarcastic and somewhat equivocal voice of that strange figure, Alcide Bava.[6] Yet we must not ignore the attraction that the coarsest savors may have, just for what they are, for the mind; and their straightforward poetic potency as well. The *peasant* who will step to the fore in the last lines of *Une Saison en enfer*, the *trader* and *settler* Rimbaud would one day become when he had abandoned words, deserve praise for lending their harsh knowledge of things to that kind of medium who dictated Rimbaud's poem: for from the eradication of qualities, from the destruction of forms, from this brutal intuition of substance, it is clear that a stormy light had broken forth, a lightning flash never before seen in the too-narrow skies of poetry.

The sarcasm of *Ce qu'on dit au poète à propos de fleurs*, its panic anti-lyricism, marks the disorganization of the old sensory approach, the overturning of the world of humanism, and for Rimbaud, the happy disappearance (yes, there is a true happiness in this savage, elusive, dancing poem) of the old self-hatred, experienced as *vomiting*, in the universal outpouring of saps. This is why I dare say I prefer this earlier poem to *Le Bateau ivre*, the other great undertaking of that summer and a more anxious ecstasy. *Le Bateau ivre* is much less the momentum of Vision than its myth; and if it manages to express its breadth and its generous immediacy, it also clearly foreshadows its failure.

It derives—and this is its only essential origin—from Baudelaire's "Le Voyage." Already a poet had wanted to test the order established by men, to advance beyond good and evil (doesn't he say so: "Heaven or Hell, what matter?") and, using words that Arthur Rimbaud was to use in turn, to plummet "the depths of the unknown to find the new." But Baudelaire, strengthened by his great capacity to love, had sought a way out by assuming his fate as a mortal being. The landscape of our odyssey, "Le Voyage" says, repeats itself, indefinitely reflecting our own image.

6. *Bava* means in French: *(he) slobbered*, and Alcide is of course Hercules . . .

We must not seek some truer reality in a mythical elsewhere, but in each being and each thing, by grasping them in the truth of their finiteness, that is, their death. Could Rimbaud understand this hope, at this moment at least? In any case, he makes this renovated myth of the quest his own and believes he will be able to announce that there is, right here, another way out. He mimes the movement that will cast the mind—once those who guided it from the tow-path, logical thought and sensory traditions, have been massacred—into the howling flood of profound colors which stretches out like a massive and stormy sea beyond the peaceful rivers. He affirms Vision as a *strength to come*, a higher life, a knowledge. Rimbaud says that he has *seen* and he *knows*. At least he describes with an inexhaustible appetite for images—the very hunger of our poetry so long a captive of the rational and the picturesque—the fermenting and circulating of saps, the waterspouts, all that moves from enormous potentiality to violent outbreaks, thunderous, rapid as lightning and broad as the deep. And these will remain for a long time—a long time in the optimistic first part of the poem—the happy images indeed, and the strongest ones, of the Unknown.

But they remain images and forms, that is, from our side of the real, nothing of the Unknown. And a doubt soon shows itself in *Le Bateau ivre* concerning the very location of that Unknown or the means to reach it *(Are these bottomless nights your exiled nests . . .)* and, even more seriously, concerning the very possibility of his quest and its sincerity. *True, I've cried too much,* Rimbaud writes suddenly, with extraordinary intelligence. The anguished wasting of oneself that, up to yesterday, the failure of love had caused, might well weaken any strength; or might well force desire to remain, far from the transsensuous ravishment, in the more modest horizon of the original frustration that is still to be appeased. Is it certain that Rimbaud really wants to go with that boat, into the bliss of these distant seas? Is he not, in this useless exaltation, rather like that *drowned man*, absent from his own ecstasy, who passes three times in the poem? Besides, Rimbaud always knows himself, he can never refrain from saying himself, and he suddenly exposes his true desire:

If I long for a shore in Europe,
It's a small pond, dark cold, remote,
The odor of evening, and a child full of sorrow
Who stoops to launch a crumpled paper boat.

What is this still water, if not the *locus* of childhood reaffirmed? And this other boat, if not a need for something else than cosmic communion, a need for love, satisfied by the slightest of things, as long as someone who loves has given it? As a matter of fact, the child that Rimbaud evokes is *full of sorrow,* he has not known that love, and he understands obscurely that the mysterious weakness of an unfulfilled childhood will hold in check within him that *poem of the sea* which he had thought to be his future strength. *Le Bateau ivre,* like so many of Rimbaud's poems, ends as the victory of lucidity over an initial swell of hope. And Vision, just conceived, may turn out to be vain: for the kind of love it unleashes, elemental, wild, glowing above the abyss, is worth less, *is* less, than the humble love of human beings which, given freely, sanctifies. Vision leads to the inner rhythms of matter, beyond place and time, and it is not certain that it can satisfy all the exigencies of a human heart.

V

We shall see these contradictions become stronger and stronger in the months to come. For the moment they appear only at intervals. Rimbaud has decided to give himself over, body and soul, to his heroic enterprise, to become *the thief of fire.*

Also, he makes himself ready to go to Paris. For in the meanwhile, between the *Lettre du voyant* and the last stanzas of *Le Bateau ivre,* crucial happenings have upset his plans. At the beginning of the summer he was alone and without much hope of being able soon to leave Charleville. A letter to Izambard on July 12 shows him penniless, even in debt (at the bookstores). And a letter of August 28 to Demeny describes his situation at home as darker yet: *The situation of the ac-*

cused: I left ordinary life a year ago for you know what. Continually shut up in this unspeakable Ardennes countryside, in no man's company, involved in an infamous, inept, obstinate, mysterious task, answering all questions, all vulgar and nasty remarks, with silence, showing myself all dignity in my extra-legal position, I finally provoked an atrocious resolution in a mother as inflexible as seventy-three steel-helmeted armies of occupation. The choice was between a job and flight. And so Rimbaud asks Demeny for advice and perhaps even support. But Demeny never replied. Did he even reply to the long letter of May? We notice an estrangement between Rimbaud and his two or three previous friends. He was never to see them again, except Delahaye, and he stopped sending them letters and poems. For their part they had stopped understanding him, at those heights to which his genius had carried him.

But Bretagne, his companion in Charleville, suggested one day that he should send his poems to Paul Verlaine, whom he had met previously. Rimbaud wrote—two letters which have been lost—and Verlaine soon answered. "Come, dear, great soul," wrote the much-admired poet. He was the first to offer to help Rimbaud in Paris, and Rimbaud met him there at the end of September.

The Word and the Absolute

I

Ah! says Rimbaud to Delahaye a few days before he left, *what am I going to do once I get there?* He wasn't very sure just how he felt. Yet once in Paris he reaffirmed, both in his poetry and in his style of living, the decision he had announced in the *Lettre du voyant.*

And largely in a spirit of purity. For there he was, "in Paris," and we must not forget the misapprehension made possible by these words. The Paris Rimbaud dreamed of was Baudelaire's Paris, and also the Paris of the Commune: the *Holy City* where poetry and rebellion revealed their identity. But the Paris he found was hardly the *locus solus* of *objective* poetry. It was much more like what he once thought he admired, along with Izambard, before more violent passions had destroyed his naïve respect for "writers." A world, and a narrow one—but he rarely left it —of mediocre, satisfied, bohemian poets who talked about Beauty and Art. Rimbaud must have hated it at once; he did not think of himself as an "artist." And if he soon seemed to be trying to find a pose, flaunting his rusticity, this was a means as well of judging and insulting pretended disorder and the illusory rebellion. "Aesthetic" complacency is the gravest of impurities. Rimbaud opposed to it, as a kind of morality, a *long, boundless disorganization.*

Systematized disorganization! Rimbaud's life in Paris could lend itself to a logic as easily as to a biography, revealing the strict cohesion of his apparently erratic behavior and of his work. *All forms of love, of suffering, of madness.* But to begin, to provide them all common ground, the destitution which was an ascesis. Rimbaud in Paris was not poor so much as passionately addicted to poverty. When Verlaine or Banville tried to help him he shunned the security they offered. He needed the zero points he found in dirty rented rooms, the moments taken from the flow of everyday life that days of hunger can procure. To these hardships add Verlaine's friendship, which quickly became an erotic attachment and threw him into sexual disorder and emotional confusion. Then absinthe, and probably drugs. *Absumphe,* at least. Rimbaud has left behind the *mugs and pints* of Charleville—simple drinks, a benign practice of alcohol—he discovers *the emerald pillars of absinthe,* its alchemical beauty of a new *green inn,* and this is suddenly the maturation, the revealed truth, the reinvention of his thirst. We know what this thirst had always been: immense, unquenchable and, if I may call it so, onto-logical; Rimbaud devoted one of his most beautiful poems to it, *Comédie de la soif,* truly a *fabulous opera* where voices from the depths are heard saying that the avid need for wine, cider, milk, cordials, tea, coffee —*Ah! If I could empty all the urns!*—is a desire to lose the self in the whirling of the saps and currents of nature, as close as possible to the great ancestors, the first children of the sun. Now, for the pilgrim of this more essential thirst, memory of the *guileless* sun, absinthe was to mark one of the farthest stopping-places, since it contains and yields up, through a miracle quite like that of *objective* poetry, a fire and a vision at the same time. Absinthe is an experience of unity. True, Rimbaud will be able later to lose interest in it, he will perceive its hateful ambiguity, perceive that alcohol is less substance than dream, less an approach to being than a resigned passivity, but for the moment he enjoys dissolving the *legends and figures* of poetic tradition in drunkenness, happy to watch the disintegration of this baleful universe of forms he was then engaged in challenging, more daringly, with a new way of using words.

For the major disorganization, the one that could claim to replace all the others, was concerned with words. Rimbaud has left a record of this whole period; it is rightly entitled *Alchimie du verbe*. And the poems he wrote then show indeed the dialectic, the wrench in the use of words, that could open them to what he called the unknown.

II

I make no claim to explain the *system* that Rimbaud implies, and which he used in the hope of saving himself from his hated condition and *becoming truly the thief of fire*. But I think that a few ideas can be set forth that will allow us to illuminate somewhat the relationship between language and poetic ambition during these months of so much discovery.

First of all, what does he mean by this *unknown* upon which his new poetics depends so directly? The letter to Demeny says clearly that it is the content of *vision*, but does not elaborate. It is then possible to think it no more than part of the real world still unexplored, or a still secret aspect of the world of appearances, but that would be to fail to recognize that *Le Bateau ivre* or *Ce qu'on dit au poète . . .* evoke objects or places primarily for the needs of metaphor, locating these *unbelievable Floridas* at the farthest confines of a breach in the world of appearances, beyond the limits of sight. *I saw the sun with mystic horrors darken:* this is more an epiphany than merely some rare sight. And when Rimbaud writes: *There were visions within those lace window-curtains,* there is no doubt he refers to something that the curtain, in "reality," is not. Yet he is not thinking of some supernatural domain. He doesn't believe in angels, nor did he borrow from the Kabalistic tradition a belief in invisible powers. He knows only *the sun, the god of fire* and *this light, nature.*

What is this goal then, that is not supernatural and is yet no part of the world of appearances, themselves the measure of everything real for so many minds? May we perhaps think that *vision* and this *unknown* have no objective value; that perhaps Rimbaud is able to be satisfied with nothing more than hallucination and dreams? There is no doubt he was quite familiar with them, and that he induced them as well. At the beginning of *Alchimie du verbe* he wrote: *I got used to elementary hallucination: I could see very precisely a mosque instead of a factory, a drum corps made up of angels, horse-carts on the highways of the sky, a drawing-room at the bottom of a lake.* These are momentary deliriums that permit the soul to become *monstrous* and to return to its true untaught nature—and it is indeed within the soul, in a sense, that vision has its habitation. Referring to the universal language to come, Rimbaud has declared that it was *of the soul, for the soul.* But we would fail to understand this fundamental realist if we thought him capable of building upon something that does not exist concretely. *A poet,* he said, *is truly the thief of fire.* And he states in *Une Saison en enfer* that at moments of highest poetry consciousness is able to dissolve itself in a culmination of reality: *I lived as a golden spark of this light, nature.*

This light, nature! We confront these words once again. And in what they suggest, which seems at the same time matter and spirit, we must recall what Rimbaud may have read in Eliphas Lévi or Ballanche about the relative value of sensory data, and about being as it exists beyond all appearance, in its unmediated obviousness. Our senses speak only of our place of exile. To recover *the true life,* the veil of the senses must first be rent. This is the true function, a negative one, of hallucinations and *deliriums.* And thus here is suggested, beyond physical aspects forced to destroy each other, the possibility of a supreme encounter which is, this time, the Vision. For Vision, in a word, is the perception, of course oblique, of course fleeting and paradoxical, of the unmasked aseity of things : this aseity which, in its stupendous immediacy, is more force than form, more ravishment than spectacle, more an eruption than a state. Are we to identify it with the "night" described by the mystics? But it is this world of ours, we must remember, that is a night for Rimbaud. When he will attempt to describe the most profound reality, the real with all its sensory degradations plucked away, he will speak of an intense brightness, of a fire in which all things dissolve, like *the little fly, drunk* in a ray of light near a country inn. Are we not sons of the Sun? *I cleared from the sky the blue which is darkness,* wrote Rimbaud. He has finally cast off the burden of sense appearances, and through Vision he enters the profound freedom of Being—a *golden spark,* from that moment on, of the *fire* that our weak, deceitful senses had denied.

Thus the *unknown* is both light and rhythm, our only true act, a *rapture;* and in any case the violent denial of language in its rational uses. For are these not connected with the world of appearances? Do they not merely describe our sensory constructions: which are precisely the occultation of being? They are not *of the soul, for the soul,* that much is sure. Yes, but it remains true (and I come now to what certainly kept alive Rimbaud's hope in poetry during these months in Paris), it remains true that this darkened language of ours still contains a spark. I say "flower," and the surrounding world is called into question. Something sacred rises up beyond our greyness. A word taken by itself becomes Word once again. So well that every poet believes he will be given by the word that which he thought real, loved, and did not have. When Mallarmé speaks of "l'absente de tout bouquet" he wants to oppose an Idea, an Archetype, to our limitations and to death. When Baudelaire evokes the Swan it is in order to resuscitate human presence in a place where nothing remains but pretense and shadows. Similarly, Rimbaud armed himself with these saving words. But he is not obsessed by Idea or mortal presence, rather, beyond sensory realities, by the substantial, luminous, rising aseity of what is, so near though always out of reach. To say the name of something, then, will be to turn towards that *unknown.* To say it seems to permit an immediate, a blind participation, in the brutal flame of what is. It will suffice that words refuse to be concepts; that they keep themselves from serving; that they disappoint man's propensity towards empirical observation in order to remain as much as possible in the light of the unnamed. And I believe I have thus defined the ambition of the *songs of nothingness*—poems that Rimbaud was soon to write— but as well of an entire tradition of poetry without any explicit philosophy, that of the simplest songs, those we so willingly call in French "transparent" when we understand that they almost burn up the dim veil of our senses. Who, in these *naïve rhythms,* in these *country rimes,* does not recall "the greenwood tree"? For here the quality of being green, as if separated from all other qualities and from its own sensorial aspects, ceases to be appearance and becomes the very face of being, in its colorless light, almost within reach. Poetry, these songs, of the mind burnt to ashes and reborn, poetry to *remake life,* initiatory poetry. It sets forth its own meaning, by the way, in its metaphors of trees, fountains, and nightingales, of gardens watched over by birds, all outcroppings of the unknown, all thresholds to be reached, and also by its essential melancholy that preserves in the very approach of the goal the feeling of still being in exile.

"Oats, oats, may summer bring you," said the old song Rimbaud kept singing in Douai . . . *May it come, may it come,* he will write in *Chanson de la plus haute tour, the season we can love.* He, in conscious poetry, is the inheritor of this aspiration to an absolute; and in *Comédie de la soif* (an *ars poetica* also) he asserts his consanguinity with the simplest songs. There is, to be sure, the world of essences, of myths that recount our nature and draw it out of time, *water-sprites, Venus,* the *Wandering Jew : age-old* since the *human spirit* has never ceased mirroring itself in them, and *dear* since despite their naïveté they have always been its resource, but *exiles* since they are nothing but images and approximate formulations. And it may be that because of this ambiguous position they help clarify our understanding of ourselves, it may be that the *spirit* who speaks in the second act of this poetic *Comedy* was right to ask them to vivify the sea, to *say* the snow, to help humanize our sojourn —but Rimbaud himself refuses to recognize in this poetry of the "spirit" either his vocation or his peace:

> *Forget these pure liquids,*
> *These water-flowers for cups;*
> *Nor legends nor figures*
> *Can soften my thirst;*
> *Songmaker, see your god-child,*

My wild desire to drink,
The headless Hydra in my bowels
That feeds upon my soul.

Songmaker, see your god-child . . . As clearly as possible, this indicates that Rimbaud's poetic thirst has been brought, through the *country rimes,* through anonymous songs, to the place of a baptism, to the threshold of a sacral life. And Rimbaud's plan is now to reach the communion that the songmaker has only suggested. His vision already beyond the realm of appearances, he uses uncertain rhythms and assonance—irregularities, broken phrases, cycles that never come full round upon themselves—to complete the confusion of this world of concepts and forms:

Age d'or (Golden Age)

One of these voices
—Angelically—
Greenly, angrily,
Talks about me:

These thousands of questions
That spread themselves out
Can lead to nothing
But madness and rout;

Remember this tune
So gentle and free:
This flowering wave
Is your own family!

And then the voice sings. Oh
So gently, so free,
And I join the song
For all to see . . .

The Word and the Absolute 51

Remember this tune
So gentle and free:
This flowering wave
Is your own family! . . . etc. . . .

And then a new voice
—How angelically!—
Greenly, angrily,
Talks about me.

And it sings just then,
—A sister of the winds:
In a German accent,
But impassioned—

The world is evil;
Does that surprise you?
Live, and to the fire
Leave his obscure pain.

Oh lovely château!
Oh life full of light!
To what Age do you belong,
Our older brother's
Princely soul? etc. . . .

I have my song too,
Several sisters! Voices
Not to be heard.
Enfold me
In your bashful light . . . etc. . . .

This admirable poem is surely the point of closest contact with the unknown, and that is why I have quoted it in its entirety. It was most probably written in Charleville; when Rimbaud went back there in May

(Verlaine had wanted a reconciliation with his wife, and Rimbaud's leaving was the price of peace). We may also believe the manuscript[1] and date it somewhat later, but still it preserves a memory of the family's house, since in it we can hear Rimbaud's little sisters talking and singing. We easily imagine him, up in his room with the door closed, listening to them distractedly. He was in the most confused period of the disorganization of the senses. Hallucinations, *magical sophistries*, as he called them, the decomposition of appearances, had become his daily bread, and it is just before he quoted *Age d'or*, in a draft of *Alchimie du verbe*, that he wrote the famous sentence about participation rediscovered. Thus, his visual perceptions were blurred. Silence seemed the adumbration of a thousand metamorphoses. But the poem came about, was formed among those shadows and lights, precisely because Rimbaud, thanks to his sisters' songs, saw appear in his fantasy just those naively poetic words which evoke so well the absolute. And, for instance, the *lovely château*, the *wave*, and the *prince:* words which, in the disorder of the mind, suddenly caused a latent consciousness to appear, vaster than the personal self, more manifold than sight, more immediate than music, a consciousness in which and through which Rimbaud's thought, but lately distinct, can imagine itself now dissolving in what is. Do not the voices speak *greenly*,[2] as if alchemically transformed into the quality of being green; are they not a *flowering wave*, *"onde, flore,"* the most fluid reality overflowing as pure light, through the "e muets" (the silent e's), just as forms space out in Cézanne's last watercolors? It is just before quoting this poem, in the draft of *Alchimie du verbe*, that Rimbaud writes : *From joy, I became a fabulous opera*. Inhabited by the very voices of greenness, brightness, of vegetation, of water, haunted, con-

1. What Rimbaud usually dated was the copy and not the composition of a poem. Thus, *Les poètes de sept ans*, which must have taken days and days of work, bears the date May 26, 1871. *Age d'or* was copied in June 1872.

2. In this context, the first meaning of the French word *(vertement)* would be *bluntly and angrily* in any ordinary use. Thus, the second meaning *(greenly)* takes on, when stressed by Rimbaud, the personal connotations he gives to the color green (cf. *l'auberge verte*).

sumed by these emanations from colorless depths, he feels the problems of the personal self disintegrate within him, and, total transparence, he truly *is*, instead of thinking or acting, as before.

I must stop for a moment before that *life full of light*, for it is to govern Rimbaud's entire destiny.

In another poem, in a tone of joyful exhaustion, he spoke of it as eternity reconquered :

> *It is rediscovered.*
> *What? Eternity.*
> *It is sea rising up*
> *With the sun.*

Which is sea mingling/with the sun, another version of the poem puts it; and it is indeed his oldest and deepest wish, this opaque world dispersed by primeval light. At the absolute height of the experience, beyond day and night, beyond time, and even hope, he would have the joy of consenting in a whisper to the desired deliverance:

> *Oh my sentinel soul,*
> *Let us desire*
> *The nothing of night*
> *And the day on fire.*
>
> *From the applause of the world*
> *And the striving of man*
> *You set yourself free*
> *And fly . . .*

At that period, wrote Rimbaud in his drafts, *it was my life eternal, not written, not sung—something like a Providence we believe in, who doesn't sing.* He started to write, after "Providence": *the laws of a world made one.* He meant a unity that consumed words, an immanent and ineffable principle which is the return of fire.

But he also says, in these same drafts, about the same poem, that he had expressed himself *stupidly*. He writes: *I thought I had found reason and felicity*, which underlines the experience of an illusion, and in the final version of *Alchimie du verbe*, he adds : *It affected my health. Terror loomed ahead. I would fall again and again into a heavy sleep, which lasted several days at a time, and when I woke up, my sorrowful dreams continued. I was ripe for fatal harvest, and my weakness led me down dangerous roads to the edge of the world, to the Cimmerian shore, the haven of whirlwinds and darkness.* Eternity recovered would consist of *noble minutes;* an illusion, nothing more. What is the meaning of such a contradiction from one page to another? And what makes it possible? But even in *Age d'or* we must now hear a certain dissonance. And first of all, in the simple fact that the poem remains, that its words have not completely dissolved in the profundity of nature, but continue to suggest a meaning, a libretto, where consciousness, and consequently the misfortune of human limitations, is still alive. And then in the very subject of the libretto. Let us listen to these voices that mingle, die away, and begin again. At the very heart of their *green* life is the fact *(talks about me)* that they are talking about Rimbaud. And if they say he has a *princely soul,* as in the initiatory tales, he is nevertheless at the same moment the *older brother,* full of dangerous and mysterious concerns which the little sisters turn away from :

> *Live, and to the fire*
> *Leave his obscure pain.*

There are the *fires* of being, or of the search for being. But there is also, as that very search *obscurely* admits, a strange torment associable with *fire,* and awareness of it endures even in the brightest moments of the vision. What is this *obscure pain?* We will have to discover it, from one of Rimbaud's poems to the other.

My sorrowful dreams continued . . . Immediately after this phrase, in the drafts of *Alchimie du verbe*, one of those dreams appears, in the poem *Mémoire*.

And certainly this poem, so wonderfully mysterious, becomes clearer when we decide that it is, partly at least, the description of a dream, in the literal sense of the word. Attempts have been made to explain it as a memory of the first time Rimbaud ran away, leaving his mother and sisters at the end of some gathering *on the mall*, or as an allusion to the earliest departure, that of his father, but all these themes unite in a more essential symbolism. *She* is the river, the Meuse that, driven by an interior darkness, by fatality, leaves the light, to wander away beneath the bridge. But *she* is also Madame Rimbaud the *Wife*, who, through pride and neurosis, has left the original current of life, though perhaps with a dull regret that the sun had vanished behind the mountain, and with it the man who could have given her a less dismal existence. Madame Rimbaud is the unmoving river. She is as well the crazed woman Delahaye describes in the first of his books, crying on the riverbank; she is as well the yellow flower, the marsh-marigold of stagnant waters; she is one who has chosen malediction and death. And in her choice she has involved her son. Upon the waters of the Meuse reappears the little boat from mornings long past, the boat tied with a heavy chain that Rimbaud, in brief moments between home and school, shook in vain:

> *Toy for this dull eye of water, I cannot reach*
> *—O motionless rowboat! O too short arms!—*
> *These flowers: the yellow one that bothers me*
> *There, nor the blue, this friend to ashen waters.*
>
> *From wind-shaken willows a powder drifts;*
> *The roses in the reeds have long since dried.*

My boat, still motionless; and its chain pulled
In this edgeless water . . . into what mud?

This is surely Rimbaud, this *motionless* boat, *tied* by his mother's unhappiness to the unknown *mud* of her neurotic unconscious. And the anguish expressed at the end of *Le Bateau ivre* is here acknowledged despite all *felicities* as a fascination now clearly understood, as an admission of defeat. In the drafts, the passages that follow *Mémoire* speak of *the black Cimmerian shore, the haven of the dead.* The words of the draft are broken, obscured by lacunae, but we can make out an *embarcation* associated with *terrors,* and surely the lost poem *Confins du monde (The Edges of the World)* which Rimbaud thought for a while to put at this place in the book, was an anti-*Bateau ivre,* a picture, beyond triumphant voyages, of a fatal path that leads to death.

Mémoire was written in Charleville in 1872, perhaps in that very month of May when Rimbaud was waiting to be able to go back to Paris.

But the same idea, the same foreboding and anguish we find as well in another account of dreams, in *Les Déserts de l'amour,*[3] which is probably a little earlier and whose emotion, in any case, seems associated with the snow and the cold, with winter in Paris. *These are the writings of a young, a very young man,* the foreword tells us, *whose life unfolded nowhere in particular; he had no mother, no country; he cared nothing for the things one cares for, and he fled from every moral law, as many pitiful young men have already fled. But so tormented was he, and so afflicted, that he only drew on toward death as toward a terrible and fateful innocence.*

Here follow *the sorrowful dreams.* And here, let us observe, prose begins to take on importance for Rimbaud as a means of analysis, of

3. It is quite impossible to accept the date that Delahaye suggests for *Les Déserts de l'amour,* the spring of 1871. In Rimbaud's emotional history these pages cannot be separated from *Mémoire* or from *Honte.* In the history of his imagination they follow the impressions of a winter spent *in the city.* From the purely material point of view, Bouillane de Lacoste's examination of the manuscript confirms the date 1872.

knowledge, and confession. More patient and more skeptical than verse, prose is better suited to express the forces that numb his heart. *Les Déserts de l'amour* have the augural beauty of awareness. We discover here that Rimbaud has preserved, during all those months of *felicity* and rapture, a most vivid sense of his enduring misfortune. Separation from *Woman*, first of all: *I was in a bedroom, in darkness. They came to tell me that she was there, at my place; and I saw her in my bed, all mine, in darkness! I was very upset and dumb—and a great deal because this was my family's house—therefore anguish seized me. I was dressed in rags; she was a woman of the world, yielding herself to me; she had to go! Nameless anguish! I took her, but let her fall from the bed, almost naked, and in my unutterable weakness I fell upon her and dragged myself with her across the carpets, in darkness! One after another, the adjoining rooms glowed red with the familial lamp. It was then that the woman disappeared. I shed more tears than God would have dared to ask.* Rimbaud goes on to say that he ran after her, chasing her in vain through a great garden covered with snow. He knows she will never come back, for *mercy would turn in its orbit more slowly than any sun.* This being that disappears, we see, is no particular woman but Love as such, love that animates all that lives, that moves the stars. It is the very principle of the cosmos, the harmony of the heavens which has excluded this *lost soul* from its eternal movement.

And Rimbaud is not ignorant either of the cause of this exclusion. It is *the familial lamp* whose approach disturbs and destroys his simple relation with reality. In *cities*, Rimbaud was to write in *Une Saison en enfer, mud went suddenly red and black, like a mirror when a lamp in the next room moves. . . .* His mother's harmful attitude has cut him off from everything real.

Les Déserts de l'amour is thus the confession of a great sadness. *At all of this I cried incessantly (. . .) In that night I wept out all the tears in my body (. . .) This time, believe me, I cried more than all the children in the world.* The phrase from *Le Bateau ivre, I have cried too much,* here reveals its origin, its permanence, and its deep roots. Similarly the child in these *Déserts* is the child at the end of *Le Bateau ivre,* the same child always longing to attach himself to another being, to a finite horizon, through the bonds of shared love. Since family, home, and country have been nothing but exile and emptiness, he would like the moment of *mercy* to give him back a place—no matter how small—in this world. This was the same love, conceived then in all its original fire, in its Panic dawning, that he had asked of Vision. But far from rekindling that fire in his life, he now understands that those *noble minutes* have only taken away all his strength, impaired his nerves, completed the ruin of his frail ability to live in the society of men and to share love with them. When he returns mute, *in rags*, haggard, from what he calls *felicity*, what resources can he still possess that might provide, in his relations with others, the self-confidence he lacked?

In other words, having tried to grasp reality as profundity and substance, he lost it all the more as harmony and communion. This is what the prologue to *Une Saison en enfer* will one day confess: this prologue in which primordial life, *the true life*, is described both as an enjoyment of *every wine*, of the very substance of being, and also—mysterious coincidence—as a communion through love. To write that, he had to understand that beauty and strength cannot arise out of disharmony. *Harmonious life*, Rimbaud had already written of the Greeks in his letter to Paul Demeny. That life of Greece had become degraded, it is true, that beauty had *one day* become *bitter*, but to rebel against their present unfortunate condition, to insult beauty in the name of the Unknown, to be hate before being love, would this really be the way to regain original happiness and love? Would it not rather be to shut oneself off even more from the great banquet one had been denied?

It may well be that poetry, though it engages us totally in a quest for unity, in an approach to the unity of being, succeeds only in separating us from other beings, and thus restores the duality we had thought dissolved. It may be that poetry can never be anything more than an impasse; that it has its truth only in an admission of defeat.

But such a truth could not console Rimbaud, for the moment at least. He was little concerned with formulating; he still thought of poetry as a way to salvation.

IV

And with that salvation in mind, sought after but inaccessible, he now finds himself caught in a horrible contradiction. On the one hand, *felicity*, a momentary illusion whose pursuit, from now on a craving, seems a curse, a vice and nothing more. *I had been damned by the rainbow. Felicity was my doom, my gnawing remorse, my worm. My life would forever be too large to devote to strength and beauty.* We can recognize in this *rainbow* the epiphany of the "colors" celebrated at the beginning of *Le Bateau ivre:* at once the unlocking of appearances, the immensity of the visionary horizon, and the hope Rimbaud had thought he could associate with this glimpse of a deeper light.

On the other hand, the feeling of an error. *Since he had not loved women—although full of vigor!—his heart and soul and all his strength were led into strange, sad delusions.* A need, then the evidence that contradicts it, and in this conflict, in May and June 1872, hesitation and disarray. Despite appearances the darkest poem of this period is surely *Bannières de mai.* A summer poem, but about summer's fierce leaden despairs, and, in spite of the blue skies and the groves of an ironic nature, path to *the black Cimmerian shore, the haven of the dead.*

Bannières de mai (Banners of May)

In the bright branches of the willow trees
The echo of a hunt dissolves,
But elegant songs still beat the air
Among the trembling leaves.
Let our blood laugh in our veins.
This place is a tangle of vines;
The sky has an angel's face.
Air and water are one and the same.
I shall go out. If bright light wounds me
I shall lie down on leaves and die.

To wait, to be bored, is too simple;
All my anguish is empty.
Let high summer dangle me
Behind its fatal glittering car.
O Nature, let me die in you
—Less useless, less alone—
Not like the Shepherds, who will die
More or less throughout the world.

Let turning seasons do their worst;
To you, Nature, I offer up myself,
My hunger and my everlasting thirst;
To quiet them I ask your help.
Nothing at all can ever deceive me;
We laugh with parents when we laugh in the sun,
But I will laugh with nothing, with no one;
And I will be free in this misfortune.

Waiting for Vision is vain, these verses tell us, and there is also the emptiness and the endless anguish of this failure. But why remain its prisoner when we can lose ourselves in time, time that kills, and accept the seasons of mortality with the dark joy of absolute despair? *We laugh with parents when we laugh in the sun,* writes Rimbaud, and this astonishing line indicates, like *Les Déserts de l'amour,* that we cannot separate love for being from love for human beings, that we cannot experience the one if we are deprived of the other—but here this idea leads to no more than a proud rejection of all love. We may consider *Bannières de mai* an ecstasy of misery, an ecstasy whose very joy is its own emptiness. A forsaking of hunger, of thirst, of all illusion and every hope— out of which a kind of freedom, in any case, will arise.

Now it may be that Rimbaud was one day to experience this active despair, this lucidity, this true, final departure. When he comes to leave Europe, *And I will be free in this misfortune,* these words may well mark the end of a phase in his destiny. But for the moment he has not made up his mind to renounce hope as clearly as he indicates here. *Oh seasons, oh châteaus,* which in *Alchimie du verbe,* precisely, accompanies the recognition that he is doomed to *felicity,* reveals something more like a kind of resignation to the present inconsistency. It's true that *felicity* has caught *body and soul* and dispersed all attempts at salvation. It has taken from *words* the coherence that might have reflected and perhaps anticipated harmony. But who can escape the desire for felicity? Of course, upon this side of the seasons and the châteaus he had hoped one day to find (they mean true life in its true place and rhythm) yielding to this desire is no more than the *flaw* inherent in every soul. Rimbaud hates himself less here than in *Bannières de mai,* he is closer to melancholy than to bitterness; during these minutes when the day is about to dawn—*ad matutinum,* at the *Christus venit*—he is close to yielding to hope once more.

Hope reappears in the open—accepted—in *La Chanson de la plus haute tour.* With a similar tone of melancholy, this *study in nothingness,* this poem close to the Unknown, is once more an attempt at spiritual biography. The *retreat,* the *patience,* the *tower:* we understand now what these words refer to: disorganization of the senses, a life that had tried to rediscover fire, but had managed only to sequester itself in an illusion. The poem describes the habit that *felicity* had created and the wreck it made:

> *So the green field*
> *To oblivion falls,*
> *Overgrown, flowering*
> *With incense and weeds*
>
> *And the cruel noise*
> *Of dirty flies.*
>
> *Ah! Widowed again and again,*
> *The poor soul . . .*

But beyond the *widowhoods (Les Déserts de l'amour* make this word easily understandable), beyond the feeling of delusion, we suddenly hear words yielding to hope:

> *Oh, will the day come*
> *When all hearts fall in love?*

and the first allusion to a new means of escaping from *felicity* and attaining salvation.

V

> *Ah! Widowed again and again,*
> *The poor soul*
> *Who has only a picture*
> *Of the Mother of God!*
>
> *Can one really pray*
> *To the Virgin Mary?*

One of Rimbaud's first *widowhoods* had been that the Virgin was for him as he says in *Les Premières Communions*, only *the Virgin in the prayer-book*, only a picture he looked at without faith. But in May or June of 1872, in his disarray, he turned to the religion of his childhood.

There is no doubt of it. *I had to travel,* he wrote, *to dissipate the enchantments crowded over my brain. On the sea, which I loved as if it were to wash away my impurity, I watched the compassionate cross arise.* This does not mean that Rimbaud found a faith, but simply that beyond the teachings of the Kabala the very failure of his experience awoke within him some of the moral categories of Christianity. *I am the slave of my baptism,* he was to say in *Nuit de l'enfer.*

He had wanted, in fact, to transcend Good and Evil, in order to regain the golden age in a violent abduction, and he had failed. And consequently he would be entitled, no doubt, like Prometheus, to describe himself, from in the humanist perspective of the *Lettre du voyant*, as the noblest and the most unfortunate of men, but he can think as well, comparing himself to Lucifer, that in such an act of inordinate ambition he had above all been guilty of the sin of pride. *All the Seven Deadly Sins*, the demon will say to him. And greed more than all the rest, a way of being selfish and possessive. I believe that from this moment on Rimbaud thought, or tried to think, that it was this selfishness that had lost him the gift of *mercy;* and I believe he began anew, seeking *a key to the banquet of old*, to contemplate the Christian idea of charity, of *selfless love.*

Should it really surprise us? I do not forget that charity (even in the vaguest sense of the word) is a renunciation of the imperious demands of *Soleil et chair*, of the Visionary's program, even of the desires expressed in *Les Déserts de l'amour*. Charity will no longer even require the approbation that Rimbaud wanted so anxiously to obtain from others when, in Paris for the first time, he acted so insolently out of his childish need to be fully accepted. But in such renunciation may not love be reborn, and is this not the most important thing? Perhaps there was once a time of glorious love, immense and yet harmonious, egocentric yet without pride. But today in the reign of Christ, *thief of energies*, is man capable of more than a kind of suffering love, altruistic and not possessive? A mutual aid among exiles, in which they might at least, by giving, escape being alone, and find again something of the *condition of child of the Sun?* I will return to these questions that Rimbaud—that *heartless*, but too loving, Rimbaud—has yet done no more than ask. It is in Belgium and in London, with Verlaine, that he will meditate upon them in his usual way, by an endeavor to live them. Then, thanks to so many admirable poems—the poems written that spring, perhaps the most beautiful in the language—and thanks perhaps to the lost *Chasse spirituelle*, he will have seen the truth of his heart.

He was working nights during the month of June that year, and they were nights filled with both anguish and happiness. *From midnight to five in the morning*, he wrote to Delahaye in a letter dated *Jumphe. Last month, my room on the rue Monsieur-le-Prince opened out on one*

of the gardens of the Lycée St. Louis. There were enormous trees beneath
my narrow window. At three in the morning the candle grows pale; all
the birds cry out at once in the trees: and that's that. No more work. I
had to look out at the trees, at the sky, held by that indescribable hour,
the first hour of morning. He makes us think of *Une Saison en enfer:*
Felicity! The deadly sweetness of its sting would wake me at cock-crow
—ad matutinum, *at the* Christus venit—*in the sombrest of cities.*

And to my description of so many anxious ecstasies and agonizing
questions, I must add still another torment, perhaps the most serious,
the one that has to do with destiny. Barely a year separates the *Lettre
du voyant* from *Les Déserts de l'amour,* but to read them is to feel that
a lifetime has intervened. The author of the *Lettre du voyant* writes in
the future tense, he is at the beginning of a program and of existence,
time means nothing to him. But the author of the foreword to *Les
Déserts de l'amour* writes only in the past tense; he sees his life as
completed. How was Rimbaud able, at eighteen, to think that his delusions, however *strange,* were final? But—and here is, by the way, the
origin of his genius, of the fervor with which he examines all the
solutions conceivable, and utilizes all his gifts in a feverish attempt to
distinguish, in Retz's words, the extraordinary from the impossible—he
must solve his problem before he leaves childhood. One who wishes to
recover from a wound suffered in early childhood must still possess the
ingenuity of a child. Once adult, reasonable, moderate, every resort is
gone. Rimbaud knew this, and knew consequently that his delusions
might soon prove fatal; for this reason was he so tormented by the
stagnation he could see within himself. Here—written out of the same
despair as *Les Déserts de l'amour*[4] but with a truly tragic self-hatred—
is the poem *Honte.* It was probably written during one of those June
nights—and certainly long before the dawn.

4. A growing awareness of destiny is expressed also in *Michel et Christine.* Would the
Visionary, after *the storm, on this religious afternoon,* be able to reach *the yellow wood
and the valley of light,* the place of reintegration into life, beside *the blue-eyed Bride?* (cf.
the *blue flower* in *Mémoire*). But *Christ* reappears to put an end to the *idyll.*

HONTE (SHAME)

As long as a knife has not cut
This brain, unfolding
White wrapping, greasy, green,
Its odor always cold,

(He, this thing, should slit
His nose, lips, ears, belly, all!
Disown and leave his legs!
A marvel!)

No; I know that as long as
A knife has not cut his head
Nor a rock crushed his thigh
Nor fire seared his gut,

As long as none has acted, this child,
This bother, this mindless beast,
Will never for an instant rest
From trickery and treason,

And like a Rocky Mountain cat
Will stink in the world's air!
Yet when he dies, Oh God . . .
Let someone say a prayer.

I will conclude under the sign of this poem. *Honte* makes clear the extent to which Rimbaud has been unhappy. I take this word in an absolute sense. And in any situation Rimbaud may find himself, in back of any idea he may try to make his, we must remember this unhappiness.

This will allow us, I may say in passing, to make no mistake about his seriousness. *Honte* was written out of those months in Paris where he was the perpetrator of so much useless defiance, so many incongruous jokes, where he let an often frivolous Verlaine talk of "luvly vinginces" and "tigerish things," where he collaborated on the parodies of *L'Album*

Zutique. All of this might pass for the games of a casual intelligence, but beneath it all, unceasingly, an anxious watch went on, and there is no doubt that, like death in the foreword to *Les Déserts de l'amour,* all of this is simply *a terrible and fateful* disguise of his true desire.

He left Paris suddenly on July 7, 1872, talking Verlaine into going with him. And it is true, if we can believe the story his companion has left us, that the journey began with the pranks of a couple of schoolboys running away from home. Yet I have no doubt that Rimbaud had made a grave decision, and that a noble plan, as important as the Visionary plan had once been, filled his heart from then on.

A Labor of Selfless Love

I

It is above all during his final months in Paris, when the quest for Vision proved so grueling and so deceptive, that Rimbaud became attached to Paul Verlaine.

Not that he had ever tried, from their first meeting, to avoid his desire for friendship. Upon his arrival, the astounded Verlaine had kept his word. When this peasant from the Ardennes *in wooden shoes* had stomped proudly into the house of his wife's parents, Verlaine had ignored the reproaches of his family and friends and had even chosen to follow Rimbaud into his dangerous experiment. He admired him, and in his company he began to drink again. He transposed into playful attitudes, with a feverish carelessness, a quest of whose gravity he was nonetheless aware. When spring arrived a little circle had formed, quite apart from "the poets" and not especially concerned with "art". Richepin was in it, and Forain, who was nicknamed Gavroche. In this small group of friends the relationship between Rimbaud and Verlaine could appear what it had long become, an actual liaison. I don't know if anyone still cares to deny the fact. There is no lack of proof, first Verlaine's letters with their equivocal and obviously delighted account of dreams and the "little secrets" he makes note of and, second, this most revealing indication, the indignation of Verlaine's in-laws and his wife's intervention, which obliged Rimbaud in March to go back to the Ardennes, where he stayed until May.

But if it is clear that by the spring of 1872 Rimbaud had long been a partner of Verlaine in what he called his *vice*, I do not believe that the affair immediately involved those acts of passion that are recorded, to the confusion of biographers, in the most famous chapter of *Une Saison en enfer*. For Rimbaud in those first months, homosexuality must have been no more than another of the elements of his *systematized disorganization*. It functioned merely in its quality as "vice," to use his term, and by that we must realize the rebellious affirmation one may make in any situation of its darker side—of opaqueness in things, of the thing in a person, of whatever rejects, sceptically and sarcastically, the so-called ingenuousness of love. For Rimbaud, frustrated and in revolt, the problem was less to oppose (and substitute) one form of sexuality to another than to oppose *vice* (whatever it might be) to all forms of feeling. And barrenness as well, and perhaps sometimes disgust, to all forms of sensual delight. Born out of his exile, his homosexuality for a long time remained merely one of its aspects—and this is why, as well, in a poetry that is always sincere, it can be so fundamental and yet so difficult to grasp. Had Rimbaud experienced it positively, it would have imposed upon him its obsessions and its values, even in the most abstract elements of his work. Experienced as a revolt, it turned him once again to meditate upon the universal. I would compare it, during these months of *disorganization*, to the "sainthood" of the convict that he had so much admired. For even the *Stupra*[1] strike a note of sad purity, despite the emotional terrorism they mean to unleash.

Besides, why should we misunderstand what Rimbaud tells us himself? If it is clear that his homosexuality has become deeply rooted, if it is also true that he did not consider it a moral fault, the fact still remains that he has described it, and not without grief, as the catas-

1. Some scatological sonnets, recently discovered.

trophe of the other love. This latter, he had always desired and had attempted. It is the *blue flower* in *Mémoire* that contrasts, near the *motionless* rowboat, with the maternal *yellow flower*. It is the *woman, carried an instant* mentioned in *Les Soeurs de charité*. *One evening,* he would write much later, *I sat Beauty on my knee—and I thought her bitter.* He had been forced to recognize a mysterious interdiction that had thrown him into *strange, sad delusions;* he will write again in *Mauvais Sang* about *the vice that since the age of reason has driven roots of suffering into my side—that towers to heaven, beats me, hurls me down, drags me on.* Homosexuality remained for him a negative passion, a deprivation, a defeat.

And yet, upon this horizon where nothing seemed possible, in this *fait accompli* of his existence, another feeling began little by little to develop.

It is already expressed, more or less, in a poem without a title, written surely in Paris, whose strange dialectic, a mingling of conscious assertion and dream, merits the greatest attention:

> *What do we care, my heart, for streams of blood*
> *And fire, a thousand murders, endless screams*
> *Of anger, sobs of hell, order destroyed in a flood*
> *Of fire, as over all the North Wind streams:*
>
> *Vengeance entire? Nothing! Oh yes, entire!*
> *Captains of Industry, Princes, perish! This we desire!*
> *Down with them! Power, Justice, History, fall!*
> *You owe us that. Blood! Blood! And flames of gold!*
>
> *Dream on of war, of vengeances and terrors,*
> *My soul! Though we writhe in these teeth: Ah! Fall,*
> *Republics of this world! Emperors,*
> *Regiments, Colonies, Nations, all!*
>
> *Who will raise whirlwinds of furious fire*
> *If we do not, and those whom we call brothers?*

Join us, legendary friends! Forget all others!
And never will we work, oh waves of fire!

Europe, Asia, America, vanish!
Our avenging advance has ravished and sacked
Towns and countryside! We will be crushed!
Volcanoes will explode! And Ocean attacked . . .

Oh friends! Be calm, these are brothers, my heart:
Dark strangers, suppose we begin! Let's go, let's go!
Disaster! I tremble, the old earth
On me, and yours, ah, more and more! The earth dissolves.

The initial idea of this poem, its explicit, or better, perhaps, its conscious thought, is that revolution and the overturning of order mean nothing now for Rimbaud, but that still he summons them, that they are even due him. Why this preservation of a desire whose object has lost its purpose? Because the work of destruction unites the rebels in a new brotherhood? Yes, but this idea seems already bypassed, as it were, by the obscure movement of the poem. In precipitous stanzas, with a frenzy that seems almost happy, Rimbaud abandons the future to an ever increasing devastation, to a fire ever more elemental that leaps from social object to cosmic object to join eventually the primitive, indifferent night in destroying the destroyers themselves. An impossible future, obviously, only conceivable in the fictitious freedom of a reverie and dissolving with it. We think, in fact, towards the end of the poem, of the most intense moments of a dream, and we are scarcely surprised to find after the last stanza, on the only manuscript that remains: *It's nothing; I'm here—I'm still here,* as if Rimbaud were regaining self-control upon awakening, with his problems unsolved.

The truth is that Rimbaud has tried by this kind of dream to resolve a contradiction he felt, perhaps confusedly but certainly cruelly. He says of his *brothers* in arms that he can at least *imagine* them such; he names them also *legendary* friends and dark *strangers,* and all this calls into question the reality of this brotherhood. The fact is that he cannot forget that once the revolution is completed, the solidarity of the period of struggle will not endure when confronted with the more difficult problems of a common existence. And so he can find no future for that solidarity except in unending civil war, which would turn a political group into a *dark*, an absolute sect. *Oh friends! Be calm, these are brothers, my heart.* This illusory solution at least makes it clear that such a brotherhood is one of Rimbaud's greatest desires.

It seems to me then, that during those months devoted to *Vision* he has also let grow and ripen a totally different feeling: a need for communion, for fraternity; the hope that if it were possible it would compensate for the absence of being that is our time's misery. This communion would have been made, not of the fire of Vision, which decidedly cannot be communicated, but—paradoxically, through compassion—of the very misfortune of mankind, at last understood and shared by all. The sentiment is Christian, though it is called to combat the evils caused by Christianity, and it would have made easier the self-confidence that man needs to reinvent other forms of love. But this hoped-for communion, too, is to be reinvented. Rimbaud in Paris had seen the shallowness of literary relations. There, he knows, man is alone. And he was also aware that each time the visionary ecstasy had failed, each time, more defenseless than ever, he needed the help of others, he could not expect to be met with genuine *charity*.

But could *he* not cause it to exist, by devoting himself to another as before he would have wanted another to be devoted to him? Could not this bond of absence and defeat that joined him and Verlaine provide the chance truly to understand another being and to set oneself free through this exercise of love? It is already a great deal if one can give when one cannot receive; and I think that Rimbaud, in a moment alluded to in *Vierge folle*, conceived the plan of devoting himself to the cause of a creature obviously unhappy, full of weaknesses, an exile and a slave—to use the words of the poem *Vagabonds*—to awaken him to the miracle of trust; in a word, to undertake his salvation. *I had*, he would write much later in *Vagabonds, in all sincerity of mind, sworn to return him to his primitive state of child of the Sun.*

Pitiful brother! Indeed, it was no passion that had taken hold of Rimbaud, but the idea of a duty and a task, beyond which, as always, he was trying to find himself, and himself alone. A task, and as always, the task of transforming a lack into a having, by challenging the never-ending curse. Since it was impossible to escape from Christianity, he would live within it, regain possession of himself by means of charity, this selfless love in which he has come to see a deadening of his own hell. Since women would not, could not, become his *sisters of mercy*, he himself would become the *older sister*[2] offering for want of receiving them, solace and love. Since Paris had been nothing but disappointment and a myth, he would also make leaving it the means of regaining possession of himself, and become once more *the wanderer I was*, nourished *on the wine of caverns and the dry bread of travellers*, as close as possible to his native sobriety. And in any case he would act, since action, for someone who has lived for so many months as a *sleepwalker*, is already a step towards those lost beginnings. *He wants to live like a sleepwalker*, says that critical intelligence that remains awake and aware through all Rimbaud's delusions. *Can his kindness and charity by themselves give him his place in the real world?*

II

But once again, the voyage did not satisfy the hope.

Too much remained predetermined in the new attempt: to begin with, the addiction to that visionary *felicity*, or at least, to alcohol, both acts of sleepwalkers, which in Belgium and London led the voyagers into the same haphazard life as in Paris. In London Rimbaud and Verlaine probably added opium to an earlier use of hashish and absinthe; it is quite possible that they frequented the Chinese taverns on the docks. In any case London is a perfect place for erratic minds. Into any pursuit

2. The text of *Une Saison en enfer* has *beloved sister (soeur aimée)*, which makes no sense. I believe this is a misprint that should read: *older sister (soeur aînée)*. Cf. "un orphelin pauvre sans soeur aînée," from Verlaine's poem "Voeu" in his earlier *Poèmes saturniens*.

it introduces its vastness, as well as the second horizon that ships and commerce provide. Rimbaud in London learned to love the idea of a new departure.

But the real reasons for failure were clearly in the plan itself; we have only to read *Une Saison en enfer*, to listen to Verlaine's voice in the chapter entitled *Vierge folle*, and we find them expressed.

Let us hear the confession of an old companion in Hell:

"Oh Lord, Oh Celestial Bridegroom, do not turn thy face from the confession of the most pitiful of thy handmaidens. I am lost. I'm drunk. I'm impure. What a life!

"Pardon, Lord in Heaven, pardon! Ah, pardon! All these tears! And all the tears to come later on, I hope!

"Later on, I will meet the Celestial Bridegroom! I was born to be His slave. That other one can beat me now!

"Right now, it's the end of the world! Oh, girls . . . my friends . . . no, not my friends, . . . I've never gone through anything like this; delirium, torments, anything . . . It's so silly!

"Oh, I cry, I'm suffering! I really am suffering! And still I've got a right to do whatever I want, now that I am covered with contempt by the most contemptible hearts!

"Well, let me make my confession anyway, though I may have to repeat it twenty times again—so dull and so insignificant!

"I am a slave of the Infernal Bridegroom; the one who seduced the foolish virgins. That's exactly the devil he is. He's no phantom, he's no ghost. But I, who have lost my wits, damned and dead to the world—no one will be able to kill me. . . . How can I describe him to you? I can't even talk anymore! I'm dressed in mourning, I'm crying, I'm afraid. Please, dear Lord, a little fresh air, if you don't mind, please!

"I am a widow—I used to be a widow—Oh yes, I used to be very serious in those days; I wasn't born to become a skeleton! He was a child—or almost. . . . His delicate, mysterious ways enchanted me. I forgot all my duties in order to follow him. What a life this is! The true life is lacking. We are exiles from the world, really—I go where he goes; I have to. And

lots of times he gets mad at me—at me, poor soul! That Devil! (He really is a Devil, you know, and not a man.)"

It is evident that the *foolish virgin* (and this is true throughout the entire chapter) thinks she hardly understands—and does not try to explain—the strange being who torments her. This is Rimbaud's irony, or perhaps his recoil before the enigma of his fate. But she will describe with unequalled acuity the metamorphosis undergone by the initial impulse of selfless love. Rimbaud may have wanted to accept things and people for what they are, but this is not so easy. *Oh dear! There were days when all men of action seemed to him like the toys of some grotesque ravings. He would laugh, horribly, on and on.* Human absurdity is too great; Rimbaud cannot assume it without trying to transform it, and his love becomes exacting: *And lots of times he gets mad at me, poor soul! That Devil! (. . .) He attacks me, he spends hours making me ashamed of everything in the world that has ever meant anything to me, and then he gets mad if I cry.* The more he had hoped to save, the more now he torments. The more he loves,—and since he identifies himself with the one he loves, the more he hates the weaknesses he finds in him. As once the quest for Vision had been, these cruel demands are nothing but a way to conceal a lasting rejection of the world; this the *foolish virgin* understands: *Beside his dear body, as he slept,* she says, *I lay awake hour after hour, night after night, trying to imagine why he wanted so much to escape from reality. No man before had ever had such a desire.*

Charity, the attempt to find his way to the path of consent, has quickly become the old revolt of Lucifer against the fact of the real. Unlooked-for transfiguration! Trying to imitate the God of love, as celestial bridegroom of a fallen soul, Rimbaud has become only her *infernal* bridegroom. Trying to save, he succeeds only in giving rise to despair. Trying to set free, he enslaves. Trying to return a man to the *primitive state of child of the Sun,* he ends up, in his blind chagrin, with a somber exaltation of depravity and death. *I listen to him turn infamy into glory, cruelty into charm,* says the companion in Hell. *"I belong to an ancient race : my ancestors were Norsemen: they slashed their own bodies, drank their own blood. I'll slash my body all over, I'll tatoo myself, I want to be as ugly as a Mongol; you'll see, I'll scream in the streets. I want to go really mad with anger. Don't show me jewels; I'll get down on all fours and writhe on the carpet. I want my wealth stained all over with blood. I will never do any work. . . ."* This disorder, this frenzy are the final convulsions of charity corrupted. And the *poor soul*, weighed down by this unbalanced affection, confesses she is both fascinated and sadly bewildered: *Ah, really, I used to depend on him terribly. But what did he want with my dull, my cowardly existence? He couldn't improve me, though he never managed to kill me! Sad, disappointed, sometimes I say to him: "I understand you." He just shrugs his shoulders.*

His charity is under a spell . . . Of course it is, and the more evidently as we know well what archetype determines both the words and acts of this Rimbaud in England, who loves and suffers at the same time. Let us listen once again to the *foolish virgin: Sometimes he talks, in his back-country words, full of emotion, about death, and how it makes us repent, and how surely there are miserable people in the world, about exhausting work, and about saying good-bye, and how it tears your heart. In the dives where we used to get drunk, he would cry when he looked at the people around us—cattle of the slums. He used to pick up drunks in the dark streets. He had the pity of a brutal mother for little children.* We remember another brutal mother, in *Les Poètes de sept ans*. And we have already glimpsed a happy childhood—a childhood granted the privilege of *pity*—in another poem of remembering which I have quoted and which I shall have to quote again, so intense is the light it sheds on Rimbaud's destiny: *Man of average constitution, was the flesh not once a fruit, hanging in an orchard? Oh infant hours! Was the body not a treasure to be unsparing of? Loving—either Psyche's peril, or her strength?* As long as the child was little, his mother was loving and the world was his; as long as he was not yet "un bout d'homme," with a questioning look and a rising awareness, she was able to devote herself to him without being impeded by her neurosis. And he too, Rimbaud, is able to really love the unfortunates and the drunkards, since they cannot meet his eye, since they do not force him to be Arthur Rimbaud before them. But before a conscious mind who understands him and judges him, before eyes that seem to reflect the sorry opinion he has of himself, he becomes once more the anxious soul, with all its moral prejudice and quarrelsome diffidence, of his harsh mother, Vitalie Cuif. Has he not decided to educate someone, as she had done? *Death and how it makes us repent,* the *miserable people,* the *exhausting work, saying good-bye and how it tears your heart:* let us not doubt that these were Madame's leitmotifs, and the first victories of her rebirth in her son.

III

Several times, at night, his demon seized me, and we rolled about as I wrestled with him! —Sometimes at night when he's drunk he hangs around street corners or behind doors, to scare me to death. "I'll get my throat cut for sure, won't that be disgusting." And oh, those days when he wants to go around with murder in his eyes! Violence, arguments, exasperations, as well as financial difficulties and mutual physical lassitude little by little dissipated the initial ideal of the children of the Sun.

A first separation occurred at the end of 1872 in order to allay gossip and to deprive Mathilde Mauté of new grounds for divorce. Rimbaud went back to Charleville for Christmas. "A horrible emptiness," Verlaine wrote at once to his friend Lepelletier. Then he fell ill with influenza and thought he was dying, and sent for Rimbaud, who arrived at once and showed the real devotion he was capable of at such times.

The next separation took place in April, and the circumstances are unclear. I am willing to believe that both thought it was definitive, though no real quarrel was involved, to judge by the bitter disappointment Rimbaud expresses in *Nuit de l'enfer,* after he revealed himself weak enough to take up a life in common once more. We may imagine as well that with springtime his anxiety had increased. He seems now torn between an obscure attraction to crime and the obsession with

Christ that we find expressed in the *Suite Johannique*. He evidently thinks already that an exhaustive reflection, carried out in solitude, would be of great benefit to him.

We know, in any case, that he went directly to Roche, the farm where his mother had settled, and it is overcome with fatigue, unable to sleep, groaning with horror all night long (if we are to believe his sister Isabelle), that he undertook the writing of a book of new intentions. During April and May, he worked day and night on his *Pagan Book*, or *Livre nègre*. In a letter to Delahaye : *My fate depends on this book*, he wrote, *for which half a dozen atrocious stories still have to be thought up* . . . It is probable that he had by then written the longest *stories* of the nine that make up *Une Saison en enfer: Mauvais Sang* and *Alchimie du verbe* certainly, and perhaps also *Vierge folle*, pages saturated with the memory of Verlaine, but where no allusion is made as yet to the outcome of the adventure, hidden still by the unforeseeable logic of destiny.

Verlaine, however, not accidentally came travelling near the Ardennes; another meeting with Rimbaud. And on May 27 the two of them left for London.

What happened? Did Rimbaud act simply out of weakness, disheartened over finishing his book, feeling that he could find nothing to substitute for Verlaine's affection?

The fact remains that from the point of view of the reflections he had begun and the experience of the past, this departure was a regression and could lead to nothing. The months that followed were to be the most violent of their life together, full of sarcasm and anger. Rimbaud could not forgive himself for having failed in his ambition. He wrote *Nuit de l'enfer*, which describes the distress of a man the slave of his destiny: *I once came close to a conversion to the good and to happiness—salvation! How can I describe my vision; the air of Hell is too thick for hymns! There were millions of delightful creatures in smooth spiritual harmony, strength and peace, noble ambitions, I don't know what all!*

Noble ambitions!

But I am still alive! Suppose damnation is eternal! A man who wants to mutilate himself is certainly damned, isn't he? . . . In the drafts we can still read : *Ah! Noble ambitions! My hate. Once again I begin an infuriated existence, anger in my veins, the life of an animal . . .* This is the darkest Rimbaud of all, during these weeks. He was doubly in despair. He made scene after scene with Verlaine, to the point where the latter, worn out with so much unfairness, left their lodging suddenly after one final quarrel and once more took the boat for Belgium.

IV

There is nothing more moving than the two letters Rimbaud sent then to his departed friend.

Moving, because we see the possibility of happiness appear, then vanish immediately, and probably forever. When Rimbaud realized that Verlaine had left him—he ran to the harbor and tried vainly, from the dock, to signal to him—he thought that this departure was the result of a true suffering, and he believed himself truly loved. Then, as never before or after, he was on the point of abandoning his mistrust and egoism and pride. Here is his first letter:

London, Friday afternoon

Come back, come back, my dear, my only friend, come back. I swear to you I'll be good. If I was mad at you, it was only a joke I carried too far, and I'm sorry for it, more than I can say. Come back, we'll forget the whole thing. It's awful that you should have taken that joke seriously. I haven't stopped crying for two days. Come back. Be brave, dear friend; nothing is lost. All you have to do is make the trip again. We'll live here again very bravely and very patiently. Oh! I beg you, it's for your own good, really. Come back, you'll find all your things here. I hope you realize now that there was nothing serious in our discussion. What a horrible moment! But when I waved at you to get off the boat, why didn't you? We've lived together for two years, and this is what it's come to! What are you going to do? If you won't come back here, do you want me to come meet you where you are?

Yes, I'm the one who was wrong.

Oh! You won't forget me, tell me you won't.

No, you can't forget me.

I have you always with me.

Tell me, answer your friend, aren't we ever going to live together again?

Be brave. Write me an answer right away.

I can't stay here anymore.

Don't listen to anything except your heart.

Quick, tell me if I should come to meet you.

Yours for the rest of my life.

RIMBAUD

Answer right away; I can't stay here beyond Monday evening. I haven't got a penny left; I can't even mail this. I've left your books and manuscripts with Vermersch.

If I am fated not to see you again, I'll join the navy or the army.

Oh, come back, I keep crying all the time. Tell me to come meet you, I'll come. Tell me; send a telegram. I must leave Monday night. Where are you going? What are you going to do?

But Verlaine was writing him a letter as well, "at sea," saying he was going to try again to get back together with his wife, this time by threatening to commit suicide. And Rimbaud answered him, his voice hidden by reasoning now, as if deadened forever.

Dear Friend,

I have your letter dated "at sea." You're wrong, this time. Very wrong. First of all, not a thing positive in your letter. Your wife won't come, or will come in three months, or maybe three years, how should I know? As for shooting yourself, I know you. You'll go around waiting for your wife and for death, wandering all over the place getting in people's way. My God! Haven't you realized yet that all this anger was as phony on one side as on the other? But you're the one who would be wrong in the end, because you keep persisting in your phony feelings, even after I called you back. Do you think life would be more fun with other people than with me? Think it over!—*Of course not!*

He had seen confirmed Verlaine's passivity and weakness, and that he needed the love of others, but could hardly give any deep affection himself. And it was nothing but Rimbaud's own weakness, in turn, his reluctance to push on to the changes time requires, that made him ask Verlaine to come back, and finally go to join him in Brussels.

I will not retell the Brussels story once more, how Verlaine, drunk, shot twice at Rimbaud who had said he was leaving. Destiny only marked the fact that a quest had come to an end.

Rimbaud was slightly wounded in the wrist, treated at the Brussels hospital, and Verlaine was sentenced to two years in prison.[3] The end, yes; the failure of the adventure of charity, the inability of an affection to become the reality of love. And, more seriously, almost the end of childhood. For Rimbaud now has a past, memories; his consciousness bears those markings that transform the virtuality of childhood into what we call "a life." Has he then to be content from this time on to obey an overwhelming fatality? Or can he still hope to get control of himself, by taking up again at the last moment and bringing to a successful conclusion the investigation begun during his lucid days at Roche, that radical and definitive work which ought already to have been his law?

He left Brussels, probably on foot, and got to his mother's house at the end of July. A few weeks later, if we are to believe the dates on the final page, he had finished writing *Une Saison en enfer*.

3. Rimbaud had never intended this, of course, nor thought of having his friend arrested. But after shooting him, Verlaine became threatening once again, this time on the street. Rimbaud got scared and sought the help of a policeman. Verlaine was arrested.

A Season in Hell

I

ᘓᘯ *Une Saison en enfer* is an examination, begun in a state of disarray but carried stubbornly and rigorously to its end, of all the metaphysical ventures that Arthur Rimbaud had attempted; and it is the search for an answer, which he intends this time to find once and for all, to the problem of changing life.

The particulars of the problem, henceforth, are three failures, each of them described in a chapter of *Une Saison en enfer*, after *Mauvais Sang* which introduces and confronts them. The failure of the venture of the Visionary, *exempted from moral obligations*, in *Delires II*, whose subtitle is *Alchimie du verbe*. The failure of the venture of charity—or of giving passion a moral substance—described in *Delires I* by the *Foolish Virgin*. The failure, finally, of the spirit of truth, when Rimbaud persisted out of weakness in the visionary disorganization of the senses he no longer believed in, or in his relationship with Verlaine after he realized it had turned into a disaster. This last failure is probably the most irritating, and *Une Saison en enfer* will condemn it with the greatest impatience, in *Nuit de l'enfer*.

But to begin, for this will be one of the main keys of the debate that commences, I think it useful to stress that Rimbaud is writing *Une Saison en enfer* for himself alone. *My fate depends on this book,* he wrote to Delahaye. He must find himself, gain control of himself, propose to his will a pact for the years to come, and one who writes under such harsh constraints is not concerned with being read. Let us accept as proof of this the great number of radical ellipses and the resolutely personal allusions to be found everywhere in these pages; also the fact that Rimbaud, who had no money, sent his manuscript to be printed. He knew he would receive only five or six copies if the book were not paid for, but that these would be enough to give this charter an objective value, a kind of personal presence in his own life.

What work of poetry, besides, has ever been undertaken in order to "communicate" a feeling, an understanding, or an idea? A poet's task is to invent and to prove true; to live, I mean, and not to formulate— he will formulate only incidentally. His clarity, therefore, goes hand in hand with his enigmas. Explicit when he must be, in order to know himself, he will yet keep to himself what he already knows. But his greatness lies, precisely, in this questing solitude. His truth shines through all his dark approaches. And if the finished poem has any value for all men, it is because its author has desired simply to be a man, in a private experience.

Une Saison en enfer illustrates for our benefit this constant law of poetic creation. Let the Poot edition, not meant for sale and yet famous, remain its symbol. It is because Rimbaud shut himself up in his disquiet that he was able to attain universality.

This said, let us turn to the book itself. It is a difficult text, as has often been said and too often forgotten, but its obscurity as such is full of meaning: it shows us the simultaneity of ideas that nothing—as in Rimbaud's life—dominates or orders in any decisive manner. For example, many of the ellipses *(Oh, my self-denial, my marvellous charity! And still here below!)* inform us that the conflicting intuitions here are much truer and more real than whatever dialectic that could pretend to reconcile them. *Une Saison en enfer* is less the formulation of a thought than the reciprocal trial of an idea and the person who conceived it, a continuous battle whose fiery violence cannot at times be distinguished from the frenzy of a dance.

What are these contradictions? Above all, now that Rimbaud has experienced his inhibitions, and the fatality of what he calls his *appetites*, his *vices*, his infernal predicament, it will be a conflict between a condition that remains so harshly and obdurately earthly, and a striving after salvation. But also—and this is very moving in a book where so much sadness with such good reason appears—it will be a desire, continually bedevilled and yet continually reborn, not to curse life. Contradictions, in a word, between energy and misfortune, between dereliction and an inexhaustible hope. As once before in *Soleil et chair*, but henceforth beyond *disorganization* and all *torments*, Rimbaud upholds the idea of *strength and beauty*, those two qualities of an existence that is able to trust itself and accept with simplicity its natural inclinations.

Besides, what would become of him if he were to abdicate his hope? He has understood—as I will try to show—that reality is doomed to contradictions, and he tries to find a place for them in his heart and his mind. So that we ourselves will have to accept these opposing tendencies, to love these storms of a violent thought. Yes, rather than to separate its terms for some metaphysical catalogue, it will be more valuable, I think, to hear their clash page after page in the book, which carries everything along in its circles and, exhausting itself without attaining a goal, brings us that much closer to Rimbaud's truth than any precisely stated idea. I shall try to lay the foundation for a running commentary of these few pages that have become, by concealing nothing of human ambiguity, one of our almost sacred books.

II

Une Saison en enfer begins, in *Mauvais Sang*, the section written first, with Rimbaud's effort to define himself in relation to other men. The feeling he experienced, so tragically at times, of essential difference— was it inescapable? Did he not have, had he never had, a counterpart?

And I must emphasize from the outset the kind of generalization he tries thus to devise. Rimbaud must have desired by identifying himself with one of the human types who limit one another throughout society and its historical development, to attain the peace of universality. He did not succeed. But this very ambition and its failure help to illuminate the rest of the book, since they place Rimbaud in his truest perspective, that of the individual who experiences his irreducible difference.

If only I had a link to some point in the history of France! Rimbaud sees—almost with our eyes, it seems—his singularity in his time, and his first thought is for those who themselves have always been excluded from history. He calls upon the *inferior* race, the race that has never entered into history's memory, since it could never raise itself above its own credulity and its instincts. *The Gauls were the most stupid hide-flayers and hay-burners of their time,* he writes. And he goes on: *I am well aware that I have always been of an inferior race. I cannot understand revolt. My race has never risen, except to plunder: to devour like wolves a beast they did not kill.* "Jacqueries," indeed, that only betray an inability as much spiritual as social. The *serfs* have let themselves be marched off on Crusades, excluded from the *councils of Christ,* abandoned by the nobles and by God. A noble is one who has found out how to become a person and who can therefore, despite his injustice and violence, understand freedom, the notion of salvation and the words of Christ. The inferior race—and here precisely is its misery—is at the same moment idolatrous and sacrilegious, greedy for God *(I wait gluttonously for God,* writes Rimbaud, *I have been of inferior race forever and ever)* and incapable of the consciousness that assures man the inner structure he needs in order to encounter God.

Thus, Rimbaud considers history in terms of salvation. He speaks of the *race* of those who have remained excluded from the heights of religious experience, and he finds now that these *serfs,* to whom God has refused the *nobility* and the *freedom* that alone make possible the idea of salvation and the confrontation of the self with the divine, are today trying strangely to save themselves collectively by identifying being with nature, and then by asking science, which has begun mastering nature, to open up the real to them. *The vagabonds, the hazy wars are gone. The inferior race has swept over all—the People, as they put it, Reason; Nation and Science.* And further on: *We are moving toward the Spirit.* There is more of Michelet and of Quinet than of Hegel in this idea of a rational elaboration of the virtuality of nature, and Rimbaud does not forget that it began under the sign, not of organization or labor (the inferior race is *laziness*), but of the irrational desire to transmute life. The science to come, because of this origin in human desires, remains an inherently religious activity. Yes, even if it is to remain also a paganism, which is all too possible if only because of the absence once again, in the communal society of the future, of the individual the serf has never known how to be, and never was.

In short, and in common with Michelet, whose *La Sorcière*[1] he had surely read and admired, Rimbaud felt that Christianity, the religion of the individual, had never really affected the obscure race of "the Gauls." Yet it would be false to think that he was glad of it, or that he could hope to find for this reason some kinship with those villeins of the sacred. Soon, we will see more clearly his double desire for a body and a soul, for salvation and for *freedom, within salvation,* for an instinctual life filled with all the happiness of immediate sensual enjoyment, but as well for deeply exploring the virtualities of the self. His ambiguity—his misfortune—is to be at the same time a pre-Christian and one who understands, acutely and hungrily, what a real advent of the individual could be, in Christianity or even beyond it. And he is now fated to turn away from this inferior race that limits him and keeps him apart *(I understand . . . and since I cannot express myself except in pagan terms, I would rather keep quiet)* but which cannot share his desire and in which he cannot recognize himself.

On the contrary, he sees, on the threshold of these modern times of ours, that the *new nobility,* the realization of the spirit through science, the collective salvation of pagan blood, cannot replace that apprenticeship of freedom proposed, begun, and before long betrayed by Christian-

1. See *Appendix I*

ity. And understanding that he was therefore (perhaps one of the last) open to what a true religious experience might have offered, he is logically enough stunned to be abandoned by God: *Pagan blood returns! The Spirit is at hand . . . why does Christ not help me, and grant my soul nobility and freedom? Ah, but the Gospel belongs to the past! The Gospel! The Gospel! . . .*

This is yet another reflection upon history. Is it Nietzsche's "God is dead"? But for Rimbaud, as probably for Nietzsche, the question of the existence of God is secondary, or even meaningless. They are both of them content with noting that there is no longer any help; that man has preserved a desire for religious individuality, for consciousness within salvation, without there being any divine hand to assist him for the last steps. Whether He exists or not, God no longer speaks. He began to form Rimbaud, but He will not finish him. Modern consciousness has reexperienced with Rimbaud the gnostic awareness of abandonment, and it is clear that when as early as 1871 he scrawled *shit on God* upon the walls of Charleville, this was more than merely an anticlerical reaction, but an attempt to reawaken the remote *Deus otiosus.*

The Gospel belongs to the past! There will be no answer, Rimbaud knows now, and he knows as well that between this silence and the anonymity of the *Spirit* to come he has only his own resources to call upon. And so immediately he begins to test them, attempting the only truly *modern* act—which is to bring sacredness into life without God's help.

III

Should we not try to detach ourselves from that struggle? Since we have lost the path to personal salvation, should we not give in to the most anonymous appetites of our race, inferior—decidedly—forever? This is what first occurred to Rimbaud.

And now I am on the beaches of Brittany. . . . Let cities light their lamps in the evening; my daytime is done, I am leaving Europe. The air of the sea will burn my lungs; lost climates will turn my skin to leather. To swim, to pulverize grass, to hunt, to smoke above all; to drink strong drinks, as strong as molten ore—as did those dear ancestors around their fires.

I will come back with limbs of iron, with dark skin, and angry eyes: in this mask, they will think I belong to a strong race. I will have gold; I will be brutal and indolent. Women nurse these ferocious invalids come back from the tropics. I will become involved in politics. Saved.

Saved! The heir of the hide-flayers and the hay-burners will have found his way back to the world of substance—to the sea, to Africa, to virgin lands; then, when he has transformed intractable nature into gold by violence, by hazardous enterprises, he will be able to impose on whomever he wishes, in the sensual anonymity of acquisition, the relations of master and slave—wherein the difficulties of Christian relations between man and woman will dissolve. It has been said over and over that this description of the ferocious invalid is a presentiment of his future illness, but I think Rimbaud is referring only to the emotional inhibition he has already confessed in Le Coeur volé or Les Déserts de l'amour. Did he not write in a draft of Mauvais Sang: If I opened my breast, would I not find a horribly invalid heart?

And yet it is possible that he wanted also to exchange one disability for another, in order to become once more through physical impotence the child he was no longer, and the object of maternal care. Yes, we may think that he came here upon the darkest of all his temptations. A man who wants to mutilate himself is certainly damned, isn't he? he wrote in Nuit de l'enfer. But then, how alive the moral consciousness of a Christian has remained in this false pagan! And what dangerous weakness there is still in his intention! Rimbaud in fact recognizes its vanity at once. What problems could he solve by relying on drugs, alcohol, or anything sensorial? A similar fantasy (in Sensation, in 1870) had not been able to protect him from the loathings that so many of his poems shortly thereafter revealed. It is in pulverizing grass and smoking that the difficulty already lies for him, since to be at ease with sensation is also an act of faith . . . But no one leaves. Let us set out once more on our native roads, burdened with my vice—that vice that since the age of reason has driven roots of suffering into my side—that towers to heaven, *beats me, hurls me down, drags me on.* In these lines probably, he cries out against homosexuality. But more profoundly as well against the theft of his heart, against what Rimbaud still calls his egoism, his loathings: the curse that will always prevent him, elsewhere as well as here, from being able to trust and to love.

Whence the new approach, if the word still has a meaning, that Rimbaud considers now: to lay waste, to destroy everything, beginning with truth; or, more nihilistically still—for terror would yet reveal a concern for *justice,* an involvement—to accept *a hard life, outright stupor; with a dried-out fist to lift the coffin lid, sit down, and suffocate.* What does he hope to escape in this way? As of now, not from his disability or its torments but from his naiveté that will not stop challenging them, that keeps hoping to be able to conquer them, to counter them with some *sacred image,* but that soon despairs and suffers all the more. It is this life of illusion, of cruel renewals, this *hell* that he depicts when he writes: *Ah! I am so forsaken I will offer at any shrine my impulses toward perfection. Horrible stupidity,* he will write in *Nuit de l'enfer* of a similar relapse. But *stupidity* is stubborn, and at the very instant he wants to destroy it, Rimbaud reveals that he remains its prisoner. *De profundis, Domine, what an ass I am!* His aspirations toward the sacred are stronger than any proofs of his exclusion. He is unable to avoid exile in the ways others have found, but cannot forget, as so many have managed, the splendor of that primeval realm.

And yet as soon as he has made this avowal of an essential conflict —and a loneliness—the tone changes, the sentences become less hurried, less broken, and if not serenity at least a new level of understanding seems to permit Rimbaud's thought to move around. The reason? Out of his very difference, out of inaptitude for the kinds of plans the rest of men devise, and far, far from those decidedly alien *races,* the nobles or the serfs, those who shaped the past or who are to seize the future, comes the awareness that another brotherhood might be able to accept him, one that had remained clandestine throughout history, the company of rebels. *Still a little child, I admired the hardened convict on whom the prison doors will always close; I used to visit the bars and rented rooms his presence had consecrated; I saw* with his eyes *the blue sky and the flower-filled work of the fields; I followed his fatal scent through city streets. He was stronger than saints, wiser than any explorer, and he— he alone!—was the witness to his glory and rightness.* Here it is, this blood which makes the outlaw, this blood unworthy of baptism, the true *bad blood* of the title, the blood that Madame Rimbaud so often blamed in her son. But he himself does not refuse this mysterious filiation. Is it not the sole source of his intelligence and his strength, which result from his indifference to the mediocre goals of mankind? *Along the open road on winter nights, homeless, cold, and hungry, one voice gripped my frozen heart: "Weakness or strength: you exist, that is strength . . ."* Here we must keep in mind the idea of the hero that had only recently been formulated by Michelet or Quinet, those two masters of Arthur Rimbaud's intellectual imagination. For Quinet, especially, the destiny of mankind depended on the unclassifiable, the rejected. "It becomes clear," he wrote, "that it is through individuals that races restore themselves. . . . They are a source of astonishment when they first appear. We do not know how to classify them; they carry war with them, and all things turn against them" (*La Création,* 1870, II, p. 252-53). But the task assigned by Michelet or Quinet to these great outcasts is a progressive, and consequently secular, agnostic, realization of the spirit. While Rimbaud, thanks to their example, becomes convinced of his strength only in order to make once more an impatient attempt at salvation.

Yes, my eyes are closed to your light. I am an animal, a savage. But I can be saved. Perhaps, in order to reactivate the original profound *strength,* it would be enough to put an end to the repression of the *savage* we are, to denounce the hypocrisies and paralysis of social behavior. Now, it seems, Rimbaud feels able to undertake the effort of transmutation before which *(But no one leaves!)* he had just recoiled. And since individual salvation is impossible, since *the Gospel belongs to the past,* since God no longer answers, he will ask the brute sensations not to bring forgetfulness as he had once desired, but to bring into the very heart of immediacy this act of faith whose necessity he had come to understand. Let the man of immediacy, the dancer, the true *savage* begin again! *You are white savages; maniacal, ferocious, greedy, all of you. Businessman, you're a savage; judge, you're a savage; general, you're a savage; emperor, old scratch-head, you're a savage: you've drunk a liquor no one taxes, from Satan's still. This nation is inspired by fever and cancer. Invalids and old men are so respectable that they ask to be boiled. The smartest thing is to quit this continent where madness prowls, out to supply hostages for these wretches. I will enter the true kingdom of the sons of Ham.* An absolute departure this time, a departure in depth, no longer a simple voyage between adolescence and retirement, but revolution, transmutation. *Do I still understand nature? Do I understand myself? No more words. I shroud dead men in my stomach. . . . Shouts, drums, dance, dance, dance, dance!* This means: obliterating any distinction between object and subject, between nature and the self; forgetting even language, which preserves consciousness, memory, and debilitating concerns for others. Then, at the very origins of the *inferior* race and in opposition to its present-day scientific ambititons, Rimbaud asserts that "religion" of instinctive fulfilment which the idea of a personal God had kept him from attaining. And no doubt, for an instant, he will try to reach this goal.

Yet perhaps he is doing nothing but miming this gesture of acceptance, and doing it in order better to recognize and define his bonds. Perhaps he wants only to relive the conflicts of his past. Already, during his visionary period, he had undergone a setback similar to the one I am about to describe, and the myth he will now put together illuminates as well his previous passage from *disorganization of the senses* to *charity*.

The white men are landing! At another time, in *Démocratie*, Rimbaud will show how concerned he is with those colonial expeditions in which the West, at this bourgeois and scientific turn of the century, seemed to succeed once and for all in the Christian annihilation of instinct. For he himself had also been colonized. And within him as well, each time he believes he has attained the elemental, the realm beyond good and evil, *the white men land* and force upon his body that *should go unclothed* the inexorable power of Catholic education. *Now we must be baptized, get dressed, and go to work* . . . Therefore, upon the very shores of the liberty he desired, Rimbaud writes a strange page where he sees himself, like a conquered black man, indoctrinated, taken in hand and "saved," if only he collaborates a little. *I haven't done anything wrong. My days will be easy and I will be spared repentance. I will not have had the torments of the soul half-dead to the Good, where austere light rises again like funeral candles.* This entire passage has a Catholic coloration which has often misled. *I am reborn in reason,* Rimbaud concludes. *The world is good. I will bless life. I will love my brothers. These are no longer childhood promises. Nor the hope of escaping old age and death. God gives me strength, and I praise God.* Is this a conversion? No, we must understand these sentences in another way. Latent yet occasionally verifiable, they reveal the expected reaction of a captive conscience, the conscience of Rimbaud the slave of his baptism, at the very moment when he would try to reopen that conscience to the primordial freedom of the *sons of Ham*. The least attempt to return to the substance of things, and precisely then his allegiance to the categories of Christianity awakens and widens, so that the two tendencies cancel one another out, leaving him in the anguish of *hell*.

As early as *Soleil et chair*, the plan for a life of the senses did not erase the memory of *that other God*. And between the *systematized disorganization of all the senses* of 1871–72 and the months of "charity" in London, between *Alchimie du verbe* and *Vierge folle*, we have observed a similar opposition, and immediately the same reciprocal annihilation of two ways of feeling, of understanding, and of loving. The truth is that this page of *Mauvais Sang* expresses not Rimbaud's faith but the power of Christianity upon him, the inescapable presence in his mind of Christian categories he hated; and it is thus a preface to the two great *Délires*, illuminating in advance their so different conclusions. *Alchimie du verbe*, we know, presents the plan of the Visionary as entirely at an end. *All that is over,* wrote Rimbaud at its close. The other *Délire*, on the contrary, does not seem finished. Although all the difficulties of charity are made clear there, the final lines remain ironically but quite clearly open to the future. *If he were not such a wild thing, we would be saved! . . . Someday maybe he'll just disappear miraculously but I absolutely must be told about it, I mean if he's going to go back up into heaven or someplace, so that I can go and watch for just a minute the Assumption of my darling boy. . . .* We find here once more the idea expressed in *the white men are landing: am I to be carried away like a child, to play in Paradise, forgetting all that misery?* And especially: *The reasonable song of angels rises from the rescue ship: it is divine love.* If nothing finally remains of the ambition of shouts and dancing, the other plan, that is the fruit of baptism, was not entirely rejected in August of 1873, and was perhaps never to be. Christian ethics were always to have the last word with Rimbaud. And it is in light of this fact that he had now to find his way.

He now knew, in any case, the uselessness of a number of efforts: *Boredom is no longer my love. Rage, perversion, madness—whose every impulse and disaster I know—my burden is set down entire. Let us appraise with clear heads the extent of my innocence. I am no longer able to ask for the consolation of a beating. I don't imagine I'm off on a honeymoon with Jesus Christ for a father-in-law.* These lines are inexplicable had we taken seriously the preceding confession of faith, but they become clear when we discover in them the double aspiration that divides and destroys Rimbaud, as well as the conviction that from now on it is vain to want to deny one of these modes of being for the sake of the other, and a clear awareness at last of what the impossible but longed-for synthesis would entail: *I am no prisoner of my own reason. I have said: God. I want freedom, within salvation.* It is important, of course, to have understood thoroughly in the depths of one's being this essential contradiction between a God who no longer saves except through moral restraint, and a nature that cannot distinguish the sacred from the instinctive—yet this first *step taken* hardly resembles happiness. It seems rather a perfect and desolate void that ought to end, as soon as possible, in death.

Indeed, the idea of death now appears for the first time in the text. And we might be astonished that it had not been pondered before— death which is a way out, which is able, in a tragic light, to grant the world for an instant to the dispossessed—did we not understand that

Rimbaud, no matter how great his courage, was not truly able to make this decision. *What an old maid I'm turning into, to lack the courage to love death!* Whoever is deprived of love, like Rimbaud, is also deprived of death. Whoever has not received the gift of having been willingly accepted, whoever has never been truly loved, cannot resign himself to dying. Rimbaud may have desired a dull vacancy of mind, abjection, crime *(A crime, quick, and let me fall to nothingness, condemned by human law):* he can never partake of this faith that death requires.

At the conclusion of *Mauvais Sang,* what is Arthur Rimbaud's thought?

The barrenness of the perspective of death confines him to his harsh life. The impossibility of salvation, the very contradiction of his religious aspirations, make of this life a place of absurdity, a stage where all things are discouraging or contemptible. *Does this farce have no end? . . . Life is the farce we all must play.* What is more, there is no rest to be found, no chance of retreat, for the punishment of anyone possessing the misfortune of desires and feelings unlike those of other people, is that he must nonetheless submit to their values and undertakings. *Forward march!* He is pushed and pulled. No matter what his interior darkness *(Ah! my lungs burn, my temples roar! Night rolls in my eyes, beneath this sun!)* and his reticence, he cannot escape this supreme misunderstanding . . . To sum up, perhaps a kind of lucidity, perhaps a state of watchfulness. But on this dark last page no future existence seems to have been foreshadowed.

By the way, Rimbaud—and I think this deserves notice—seems nowhere in this entire chapter to have attempted to modify (I no longer say: transmute) his unhappy condition. For instance, psychological reflection, the necessary beginnings of a cure, is absent from *Mauvais Sang.* As well as all social criticism. The passionate supporter of the Commune, who in the spring of 1871 wrote a Proposal for a Communist Constitution, seems now uninterested in the political conditions necessary to change life. But we have seen him, on the contrary, evoke the disorderly, credulous masses who made possible the Crusades—and there is a great deal of meaning in this. The revolutionary seeks to modify the facts—psychological or social—and improve on them, while the Crusader wanted to transfigure them; and so, despite an early naive hope that had vanished with the Commune, the Crusader is Rimbaud's real ancestor. *Mauvais Sang* is concerned with salvation, not with a cure. It is a phenomenology of the entrapped conscience: photographing its sudden hopes, its flights and despairs, but only in order to maintain our mind on the threshold of miracle and grace. And rather than to come to partial remedies, relative solutions, we see clearly that the author of *Mauvais Sang* prefers to remain on the elevated plane of impossible resolutions, vanished virtualities, in order to retain a shadow at least of the true draught, and thus to dwell, even if in his customary abrupt manner, "poetically on the earth."

IV

But all this had not taken into account a certain weakness which had never been repaired and which, the moment these pages were written, became nonetheless the stronger reality and ruined for a moment the very ambition of *Une Saison en enfer*. *Mauvais Sang* was written in May. Several weeks later, in London, *Nuit de l'enfer* bears witness to a relapse. When he writes: *I was close to a conversion to the good and to felicity, salvation,* it is possible that Rimbaud is alluding to drug experiences. Everything leads us to believe that together with Verlaine he smoked hashish or opium at different periods during his life in England. And we now know how much he could detest anything that promised paradise and brought nothing but the evils of habit. And yet, when in anger and anguish he describes the bad outcome of the experience, it is clear that he sees in it something far more serious than simple disappointment. *I have just swallowed a terrific mouthful of poison.—Blessed, blessed, blessed the advice I was given!—My guts are on fire. The power of the poison twists my arms and legs, cripples me, drives me to the ground. I die of thirst, I suffocate, I cannot cry. This is Hell, eternal torment! See how the flames rise! I burn as I ought to. Go on, Devil.* Indeed, whatever the poison had been, and because he begins again, because Rimbaud reveals himself incapable of saying no to its seductions, we must understand it as the obstinacy of hope. And it is precisely this, this everlasting naiveté, that exasperates the author of the last pages of *Mauvais Sang.* Once more, upon his return to London, began a life of exhausting *felicities,* of emotional drifting and bitter disillusionment. Rimbaud thought he had attained a lucidity, a knowledge, but the slightest of allurements has imprisoned him anew in the *hell* of absurd hopes and their terrible awakenings. Was he then incapable of obeying the truth? He had finished the picture of his metaphysical condition; is it possible that obscure necessities, this time psychological, prevented him from remaining its incorruptible witness? *And to think that I possess the truth, that I can have a vision of justice: My judgment is sound and firm, I am prime for perfection. . . .* The unhappiness of *Nuit de l'enfer* feeds primarily on this weakness. But Rimbaud's energy refuses to accept it. So, after having believed in the early part of this book of vacillating wisdom that he had freed himself from hope, he is going now to search for what deep reason he remains entrapped within it.

Nuit de l'enfer, then, attempts the psychological analysis that *Mauvais sang,* remarkably, did not. In the perspective once again of *Les Poètes de sept ans,* and with the undiminished violence of *Les Premières Communions* Rimbaud turns to his childhood in order to accuse Christianity of having condemned him not only, as he had a short time before understood, to the illusions of good and evil, but also to the torments of an indestructible hope. *I am the slave of my baptism,* he now writes bitterly. It is the Savior's religion that has taught him the notion of another, truer world, and with that promise condemned this world here to nonexistence. *The clock of life stopped but a moment ago. I am no longer within the world.* And again: *I believe I am in Hell, therefore I am.* Christian hope for Arthur Rimbaud is not an arguable premise of metaphysical speculation. It is a poison that from childhood *(You, parents, have ruined my life. . . .)* has subtly disincorporated the real world, replaced man's relationship to existence with hallucination and fantasmagoria, and destroyed all authentic ontological experience, in place of which there is nothing more today than ephemeral resolutions, weariness, *all the ugly faces I can make,* and finally nothing but the art and the gratuitousness of the actor . . . In all of his work, Rimbaud revealed himself obsessed with the actor who is so busy within him: who plays the *comedy* of truth without really being able to live it. And in *Nuit de l'enfer,* he sets upon the empty stage of the world that *talent* which he possesses all too much and wherein he finds the true symptom of our alienated condition. *Listen! Every talent is mine!—There is no one here, and there is someone: I wouldn't want to waste my treasure.—Shall I give you Africk chants, belly dancers?* A world—and the history of modern art will prove him correct—where one can have the *talent* to imitate the style of black art, but not the strength to recreate the substantial life of the *sons of Ham.*

Nuit de l'enfer compared to *Mauvais Sang* thus reveals a profound change of perspective. In the first chapter an "absolute" consciousness acknowledged its contradictions, took cognizance of its limits, suffered from its inability to overcome them, but could conceive itself only in terms of its own difference and solitude. It was as far from the serfs as from the nobles, from the West as from the pagan societies, as if it had been born along with life itself in order to bear witness to it, without having at any moment undergone the slightest historical influence. The quest for some counterpart in history ignored the course of historical development, with its accidents full of consequence, and prevented an analysis of the immediate causes of the present disorder. And if the dominion of Christianity was admitted, and was all the more suspect because it was accepted without faith, no question was asked in what necessary or contingent way it asserted its authority. *My heart has been stabbed by grace,* wrote Rimbaud. Yes, that might have been an authentic element of metaphysical torment, a limit that any man must fatally encounter, even if no deliverance follows. But to this description *Nuit de l'enfer* opposes a psychology and a critical method. Somewhat Marxist and pre-Freudian, these pages uncover the unconscious, the subterranean movement of ideas, the fetters of a mind that had thought itself free—everything that might be contingency and *poison* in the development of the spirit: that Christianity is a sickness of the soul; that hope, condemned but mysteriously alive once again, is disturbingly connected with this destructive religion; and that Rimbaud's future is inescapably predetermined, since, as a *slave* to the moral and spiritual structures of a religion and a time, he no longer has even the power to attain what he still desires and holds true.

This man, here and now, Arthur Rimbaud, has become in his own eyes the true subject of reflection. So it is logical that in the *Saison, Nuit de l'enfer* is followed by the two most searching portraits that Rimbaud has left us of himself, *Alchimie du verbe* and *Vierge folle*, interrogations, this time, quite concrete and personal, of his momentary hopes and his lasting failures.

V

But no matter how important the details of this complementary analysis, it does no more than to illuminate two specific forms of the alienation he has denounced, and I will not go back over these pages that I have already tried to understand. Rimbaud in *Une Saison en enfer* is concerned with his future, not his past, and we must look beyond the two great *Délires* to pick up the traces of the thought in progress in which he involves his destiny.

The progress begins again in the first words of *L'Impossible: Ah! My life as a child, the open road in every weather; I was unnaturally abstinent, more detached than the best of beggars, proud to have no country, no friends—what stupidity that was!—And only now I realize it!* I believe Rimbaud must have thought thus, spoken thus, while still on the road between Brussels and the Ardennes, as he returned wounded and shaking with fever from his last adventure. And I take this stupidity, so nobly and purely denounced, to mean his former hope of salvation and the lack of interest in earthly goals that accompanied it. Rimbaud now knows, as we have learned, that he is condemned to this hope; that it is his *vice* as much as it is his virtue; that it is vain, except that it permits him to escape universal meanness—and he begins to think of a new aim. If it is true that any metaphysical resolution will be vitiated by hope, why not undertake to scorn hope's desires, and thus to avoid this most formidable *demon* of all? No longer those *departures* of *Mauvais Sang* whose only concern was salvation and which remained trapped in religious alienation; but to say *to hell with martyr's palms, all beacons of art, the inventor's pride, the plunderer's frenzy,* and thus to escape from the *subtle, stupid torment* of soteriological speculation and rediscover the fatalistic, almost immobile wisdom of the *Orient. I am running away!* But if Rimbaud believes he has recovered *two cents' worth of reason,* he tells us too *how quickly it goes,* and in fact he soon falls again under the influence of the categories he was trying to avoid. For what, in fact, does he mean by *wisdom?* There are precisely men of the Church to explain it to him. *True enough: it was Eden I meant,* it is still the longing for life transformed, returned to its original glory, it is only an avatar of the dream of salvation. Barely has he renounced his *spiritual ramblings* than Rimbaud begins once more to assert, for example, the integrity of *movement, form,* and *light*—the excellence that is still virtual in the real —the possibility of its, and our, salvation.

Careful, mind. Don't rush madly after salvation. Train yourself! But how difficult is this discipline when the mind is in fact *asleep!* There is no attempt at evasion that a lingering hope will not try to manipulate. *Human labor,* belief in the principles and the development of science, the only truly secular plan, is put aside because of its slowness, wherein all possibility of a miracle is lost. Laziness once again, and a life of poetry and reverie, immediately betray their deceptive purposes: *Acrobat, beggar, artist, bandit—priest! On my hospital bed, the odor of incense came so strongly back to me; guardian of the holy aromatics, confessor, martyr.* . . . Rimbaud perhaps wanted only, in these pages of *L'Impossible* and *L'Eclair,* to verify forever the fatality so painfully experienced in the chapter on his London life. But this time he comes full circle. The *impossible* is quite evident. It is now clearly established that a *filthy childhood education* has given this life over to incessant revolt and to a pride as vain as it is destructive.

And it was Hell, writes Rimbaud in *Matin; the old one, whose gates were opened by the Son of Man.* The one that permitted no escape, under the dark sway of Law.

And now before us, truly, lies the darkest page of the book, the one which might have been the renunciation and the end. The night begun so long ago, the night lit for a moment by lightning, is from this point on totally black, and in no way can we imagine the coming of day. And yet—and surely we have to discover in this the most secret intention of the work, its noblest moment of unconquerable energy—it is this moment of darkness that Rimbaud has chosen to call *Matin* (Morning).

He refuses to forget that this life, today so vitiated and paralyzed, may also be, as he once said in *Soleil et chair,* glorious and pure. *Hadn't I once a youth that was lovely, heroic, fabulous—something to write down on pages of gold?—I was too lucky!* He refuses also to try vainly to forget his present weakness, the other term of the contradiction in his thought. But in the space between them, and this time without anger, he consents to the incessant rebirth of the illusion of hope. *From the same desert, towards the same dark sky, my tired eyes forever open on the silver star, forever; but the three wise men never stir, the Kings of life, the heart, the soul, the mind.* His voice now is the gravest and the purest of all, when he gives consent to this destitute hope. For he is now able to call it a star, even if the gold of the highest transfigurations does not shine from it, even if the saviour will never appear.

I really believe that Rimbaud, in this hour before dawn, was converted to hope. And by that I mean he now understands that the circle he calls his *hell*—impatience, impulsive outbreak, disillusion, bitterness—is identical, being unquenchable and anxious, with life, and that, as far from his former credulity as from the ataraxia he so vainly desired, it must be recognized as the only reality in this universe of lack. Consequently he, Rimbaud, must accept its "lies" and its ravages, yield to it as a boat yields to the waves of the ocean, respect it, and love it. A yielding to the unresolvable contradiction, this true awakening from the sleep of Western illusions that Rimbaud had already glimpsed in *L'Impossible* and had called *wisdom* and *purity*.

In *Adieu*, which follows *Matin* and closes *Une Saison en enfer*, Rimbaud repeats his consent to what is today the essence of man, no matter how divided.

Yes, all the contradictions experienced in the tempestuous course of the book are maintained, as in *Matin. Autumn already!* the absence of an *everlasting sun*, the seasons of death where man's finiteness is revealed through his temporal limitation, *poverty's harbor*, that human location so decidedly earthbound—even when we can perceive a glow in its sky. On the other hand, the inexhaustible desire for the absolute of those forever engaged in the *search for divine brightness*, and that illusion as tenacious as vain which causes Rimbaud, the disappointed, the "desperate," still to write: *Sometimes in the sky I see endless sandy shores covered with white rejoicing nations*—the eternally deceptive mirage of the *true life*. Between the fact and the hope, no communication, actual or possible. *I thought I had acquired supernatural powers. Ha! I have to bury my imagination and my memories.* But this aporia must no longer be a source of complaint. *But why regret* (...), writes Rimbaud. Better to welcome in it an arid yet salutary occasion for truth.

I! I who had called myself a magician or an angel, free from all moral constraint . . . I am sent back to the soil to seek some obligation, to wrap gnarled reality in my arms! A peasant! Just as the *peasant* never dreams of avoiding the material fatality of earth, so we must no longer seek to deny, in our divided situation, the spiritual fatality. Such is our condition in the *new era*, which will be the era of truth.

And thus, at the conclusion of *Une Saison en enfer*, Rimbaud leads Western man to the conclusion of his history. For in the ambitions and dreams, the myths, the too easily accepted *deliriums* of the Christian centuries, he denounces a credulity which is our greatest alienation, but he refuses as well to let our spirit resign itself, and he even proposes to it, beyond religious fantasmagoria, the task of a realism, in the existential meaning one may give to the word. *One must be absolutely modern,* wrote Rimbaud. For him, it would seem, the problem of alienation is not in the final analysis political or economic, but moral. Man alienates himself when he becomes impatient and yields to his dreams, because he thus loses an awareness of his limits, when these are the foundation and the approach to his most profound reality. Modernity is the *peasant's* grasp of a world untouched by miracles, of a difficult but healthy duality in the condition of man, misery and hope at the same time. And the future will not be one of possession or glory but truth, for the obsession with salvation or its equally vain disavowal will finally yield to this creative recognition: that we exist only in this desire, that never obtains and never relents—our eternal struggle with finitude, far from the discouraged and far from the credulous, *far from those who die as seasons turn.*

VI

But what is to be the vehicle of this new realism? And must I not offer further proof of the reversal of values I think I perceive in *Adieu?*

I would have hesitated, in fact, to risk this interpretation were there not on the last page of the work at least one possibility of cross-checking. It is true, this page is particularly secretive, discontinuous, and elliptic; it is as if Rimbaud hesitated to write everything down, and knowing that the latent presence of an idea is more creative than its formulation, as if he wanted to deliver to himself a sybilline message. But let us pause before a word that reopens a perspective, and which possibly illuminates the most profound aspect of the plan.

Immediately after setting his task in the future, *to wrap gnarled reality in my arms,* Rimbaud writes: *Am I deceived? Would charity be the sister of death, for me?*

In his new plan, then, charity has a part. And if we go back now to the prologue of *Une Saison en enfer,* which was probably written after the book, and which seems anyway to assume that it is already finished, we can make use with greater assurance of another allusion that Rimbaud makes to this half-hidden idea. *Now recently,* he writes, *when I found myself ready to croak, I thought to seek the key to the banquet of old, where I might find my appetite again.* Immediately following, he adds: *That key is charity.* Are we not justified ourselves in making a key of it, a key to the silences of *Une Saison en enfer?*

And I think it will be enough for me to recall now a sentence from *Vierge folle: Can his kindness and charity by themselves give him his place in the real world?* as well as the memory of that labor of *charity* that had for a time brought Rimbaud close to the weak Verlaine, and the path will appear that even now he intends to follow toward acceptance of reality. When he had decided to restore Verlaine to *his primitive state of child of the Sun,* to recover within the world of Law the lost plenitude, he had already sought the help of a love of things and beings such as they are; and clearly his model, in that hell *whose gates were opened by the Son of Man,* had been the new love for human weakness that Christ introduced into the world. But self-hatred then had forbidden him the love of others. Let us not however forget that this *delirium* in *Une Saison en enfer* has no conclusive ending. The Foolish Virgin says only: *If he were not such a wild thing, we would be saved.* And again: *Someday maybe he'll just disappear miraculously.* Although it is evoked with irony or perhaps modesty, the *assumption of my darling boy* was no doubt a difficult idea to forget, and it may well remain the great plan that *Adieu,* in a more resolute tone this time, and with an ambition more restricted and lucid, still intends to carry out.

I think so, in any case, and that Rimbaud in *Matin* and *Adieu* has simply tried to apply to himself, for acceptance of himself—acceptance of his hope, but also of his *stupidities,* his *vice,* of all that the poem *Honte* had once so cruelly condemned—the creative power that is to be found in charity. To be for oneself the Son of Man who delivered mankind from sin by giving His love, to accept oneself as one is, imperfect and incomplete, thus to dissolve pride and the drive to possess and the impatience that can so profoundly cut us off from reality—do all this, and the acceptance of hope that I have tried to describe will take root in a richer soil. Charity is the *glowing patience* that will convert adversity into responsibility, suffering into being, *the dead bodies who will all be judged* into that possible vigil whose dawn will see the advent of truth *within one body and one soul* in an existence reborn.

And, last, it is charity, thus identified with the duty of man and historical modernity, which accounts for the resolute decision of solitude we find at the conclusion of the book. *Why did I talk about a friendly hand!* Rimbaud writes. *My great advantage is that I can laugh at old love affairs full of falsehood, and stamp with shame these deceitful couples . . . I saw women's hell over there* (. . .) In vain had he asked woman to be his *sister of charity;* he now takes the place of all others, in a world clearly without resources, with the aim of understanding and reviving his own self. He alone must call down the moment of *mercy* from the empty sky. Like the convict and the saint, he must accomplish by himself his great task, the reinvention of love.

And yet how strange it is to see charity and solitude asserted in the same instant! Is the barely perceived reality not once more fading from view, is not this alleged sufficiency of the self simply Rimbaud's former *pride,* former *demon,* active again? Egoism once more, instead of faith? And from another point of view is it not dangerous to identify charity with the search for reality, if it is true that reality is as much what might happen as what is, as much nature as the self, as much a legitimate object of science as an occasion for patience, even when the latter becomes a creative ascesis through the new will to love? Once before in Western history charity partitioned existence, and ended far from human needs.

We know that Rimbaud in *Adieu* did not hesitate to express a feeling of victory. *For I can say,* he wrote, *that I have gained a victory; the gnashing of teeth, the hissing of the devil's fire, the stinking sighs subside. All my monstrous memories are fading.* But he says as well, and he knows as well, that his struggle is not over. It is still no more than a *watch by night,* not yet the morning. *Never mind hymns of thanksgiving: hold on to the position I have won. A hard night! Dried blood smokes on my face, and nothing lies behind me but that repulsive little tree!* The tree, the sterile and accursed tree of good and evil is always dangerously present in the mind of the Rimbaud who hoped to go beyond Law in the creativity of love.

And, still more clearly, hardly had he written in the prologue: *That key is charity*, than he adds: *This idea proves I was dreaming!* "*You will stay a hyena, etc. . . . ,*" *shouts the demon who once crowned me with such pretty poppies.* "*Seek death with all your desires, and all selfishness, and all the seven deadly sins.*" It is true, charity may be the *sister of death* if it eventually moves further apart from other beings someone whose sin and whose complaint was precisely that he was set apart; and as well if it turns him away from the possible, from nature, when his own nature is still so demoniac and undeveloped.

Let us leave Rimbaud, however, out of regard for the uneven progression of subjective quests, to this new concern to give himself a task, a goal, even at the risk of deceiving himself. No doubt, after months of darkness, it is a great deal to have recovered the richness and the vitality of a decision. His desire to live has revived. Solitude, which was a fact and seemed to be a dead end, has become, through the usual dialectic of poetic energy, a possible means of transmutation of a joyless condition. And society is no longer so desperately alien, since Rimbaud can claim to serve as its vanguard in the struggle for modernity.

I will limit myself, in conclusion, to this. It has often been set forth that *Une Saison en enfer* condemned poetry, at least turned away from it, and I make no objection. *Art is stupidity*, it says in the drafts, without equivocation. Inasmuch as it was a tool of defiance, the resource of illusion, a dreamlike idea of salvation, poetry has hardly a place in the time of patience to come.

But will Rimbaud remain unshakeably faithful to his difficult (and contradictory) intention? Will he not once again obey his *dear Satan?* I am thinking now of the final lines of the prologue—these last moments, perhaps, of the summer's reflections—where already he foresees *a few belated cowardices.*

Illuminations

I

℘ Until now I have not wanted—noticeably, perhaps—to examine too closely or to quote from Arthur Rimbaud's prose poems, the *Illuminations.*

The reason is that the date of their composition has not yet been determined with sufficient precision. It is true that Rimbaud does seem to reject poetry in *Une Saison en enfer,* and scholars and biographers have therefore long been convinced that all of his writings without exception antedated the summer of 1873. But a few facts, which I shall return to, seem to guarantee that at least two or three of the disputed poems were written after *Une Saison en enfer.* And there is nothing in the realm of material evidence to prove that any of them had even been begun before his great attempt to deny poetry.

It was thus necessary, I thought, to set this enigma aside, to examine the *Illuminations,* if not as a whole, at least as a single problem, and to find out whether the perhaps varying moods of these poems coincide or not with different aspects, now perhaps more explicit, of Rimbaud's thought. Some conclusions seem possible. If we never forget, of course, the obscurity in which we are forced to proceed.

There are so many aspects of Rimbaud's life, of his thought and of his work which are still, and some which will remain forever, unsure or undecipherable! I want to emphasize this at the very beginning, simply to awake a useful attitude of suspicion.

For example, what do we know about the *Prières* that Verlaine mentioned in 1872, the *Chasse spirituelle,* so often discussed and still lost, or *Esplanade,* which the same Verlaine asked Rimbaud to send him while the latter was writing at Roche, in May, the first sections of his *Pagan Book?* The greatest part of his early prose work has disappeared, probably forever.

And, the gap is almost as serious, what do we know of Rimbaud—the encounters, the friendships, the books he read—during those fifteen or eighteen months, clearly so decisive, that followed *Une Saison en enfer?* Did they not witness events which, if they were known to us, would compel us to consider them indispensable landmarks? Why did Madame Rimbaud, who travelled very little, come to London in June 1874? In another connection, when we read *Vies, II* or *III,* poems that are obviously autobiographical, are we certain that we understand every allusion? *I am an inventor,* writes Rimbaud, *much more deserving than all who have preceded me; a musician, even, who has found something which may be the key to love.* Even if we compare these lines to the prologue of *Une Saison en enfer,* and to the idea of charity, which was once the *key* to love, they remain obscure because of the reference to some kind of music. Was there not once a Rimbaud, too little remembered today: the one who loved—or wrote—an *Ariette oubliée (words and music),* who read Gautier's *Club des Haschischins,* and who reflected upon the role of the "voyant"[1] as a dispenser of music; a Rimbaud who would later want to own a piano, the Rimbaud of the *childish music* denounced in *Nuit de l'enfer,* a feverish, strong, speculative mind, quite capable, after all, of reviving the categories of Pythagorism or of Orphism through some naive attempt to shape a *new harmony?*

1. The "voyant" did not smoke hashish, because he had to play the piano, for the benefit of those who did.

Again in *Vies, III,* he writes: *In an old alley in Paris, I was taught the classic sciences.* Remembering that out of seriousness and concern for truth Rimbaud hardly ever mixed fantasies with the facts of his existence, I confess I am tempted to give that sentence a literal meaning, in order to compare it to others that are just as mysterious, and not to dismiss the idea of some belated initiation: *I am a scholar in a dark armchair—branches and the rain beat at the casement of my library (Enfance). What did they do with the Brahman who taught me the Proverbs? (Vies, I). To this holy old man, hermitage or mission (Devotion). Let there be no one here below but one old man, beautiful and calm, surrounded with "unimagined luxury" . . . I will be at your feet (Phrases).* This *"unimagined luxury"* takes us back to *Vies, III: In a magnificent house encircled by the Orient entire, I brought my life's work to completion, and I passed my illustrious retirement.* The allusion is probably to drugs, to hashish and opium, whose seductions we will see made more apparent in several *Illuminations,* but that cannot be separated, it seems, from a teaching and a method that nothing in Rimbaud's known life gives us grounds for discussing. What encounters did he make during the fall of 1873, during his new stay in Paris? I keep imagining *an old alley*—le passage d'Enfer, so close to where Rimbaud lived; the endless propositions the city has to offer, and his tireless imagination. A mediocre portrait, painted also very near the rue Campagne-Première, and probably during these same months, shows Rimbaud in a profound sadness, as far as possible from the heroic spirit that moves the final pages of *Une Saison en enfer.*

In both dimension and duration, Rimbaud's experience surely goes beyond the temporal and intellectual framework—from the *Lettre du voyant* to *the truth in a single body and a single soul*—to which, in our ignorance of the facts, we might be tempted to reduce it. And we must keep in mind this sense of what we do not know if we are to study the final prose poems without disastrous presuppositions.

II

What we know for certain comes down to a few facts.

First, the date of the manuscript. A comparative study of the hand-writing has proved that a great many of the poems were recopied in the spring of 1874, several months after the printing of *Une Saison en enfer*. It is just at this moment that Rimbaud reappears. He is in London, with the poet Germain Nouveau.

But that the poems were recopied in 1874 does not prove that they were written in that same year. More important are a few clues that seem to establish dates for some of them, and which also indicate a late period. The utmost probability attaches to the influence of Flaubert's *Tentation de saint Antoine*, published in April 1874, upon *Barbare*, *Enfance, I*, and *Villes, I* and *II*. In *Aube*, the use of the word *Wasserfall* has been emphasized as relative to the study of German, which Rimbaud only undertook seriously in the final months of the year. I will consider above all two facts that are hardly questionable. One of the poems, *Vagabonds*, recounts the adventure with Verlaine with such evident detachment and distance *(Pitiful brother! What atrocious sleepless nights he caused me!)* that it can hardly have been written during the more violent months of *Une Saison en enfer*. And in *Jeunesse*, where explicit reference is made to the *temptation of Anthony*, one of the parts of the poem bears the title *Vingt ans* (Twenty Years Old). *How the world this summer was full of flowers!* Rimbaud remarks. Does he not write this fragment in the fall of 1874 a few months after the publication of Flaubert's book, when he himself has just turned twenty?

So there are two poems at least that to all appearances were written considerably after *Une Saison en enfer*, and we are thus justified in thinking that Rimbaud, despite his clearly stated renunciation, has returned to poetic creation. On the basis of these data, I shall risk a few hypotheses.

And first, I will separate from the ensemble of the *Illuminations* three or four poems that seem to me closely linked to *Jeunesse*, and thus form a group that can make clearer a certain period in Rimbaud's thought. *Jeunesse* itself is a very important poem in its biographical indications. In it, Rimbaud turns again toward a time that seems far away, and his understanding of life here seems more mature and even more resigned than in his other writings. But these same traits are to be found in *Vies (I, II, III)* and in the poem *Guerre*. In each of them we find the same unappeasable memory, the same obsession with an ambiguous *at present* divided between hope and failure:

At present, gentleman of a bleak countryside beneath a frugal sky, I attempt to awaken my feelings in the memory of a wandering childhood, of my apprenticeship, my arrival in wooden shoes . . . of polemics, of five or six widowhoods, and of several wild nights where my hard head kept me from reaching the exaltation of my companions. I do not regret my former share of divine gaiety; the frugal air of this bleak countryside fortifies very effectively my atrocious scepticism (Vies, II).

At present, the eternal inflections of the Moment and the infinity of mathematics hunt me over this earth where I experience all civil successes, respected by strange childhood and enormous affections (Guerre).

At present, with this toil completed, you, your calculations, you, your impatience . . . (Jeunesse, II, Sonnet).

Let us pause before this *at present* that Rimbaud himself is aware of, and let us try to discover what it meant for him.

He tells it to us, perhaps, in *Jeunesse* once again: *all calculations set to one side, the inevitable Descent from Heaven, a visitation of memories and a seance of rhythms invade the house, the head and the world of the mind.* This sentence, at the beginning of a long poem, in the calm hiatus of an English *Sunday*, before turning once more to his *study:* well may we imagine that it reunites and intends to reunite all the elements of his thought. And this thought may be somewhat incoherent, or even contradictory: let us guard against trying to understand it too soon. But let us compare these *calculations*, for example, with other allusions scattered throughout this group of poems.

Thus, *Jeunesse, II* states that *you, your calculations, you, your impatience* are not more than *your dancing, your voice,* and that these are reasons *for a double occasion of invention and success.*

Then, in *Jeunesse, IV* we read: *But you will undertake this task; all the possibilities of Harmony and Architecture rise up about your seat.* And in *Guerre,* where the *infinity of mathematics* is also invoked, a *war, by right or by force, of a logic quite unexpected* is said to be—it would seem—*as simple as a musical phrase.* This time we think again of the sentence from *Vies, II: I am an inventor much more deserving than all who have preceded me: a musician, even, who has found something which may well be the key to love.* In each of these sentences, undoubtedly, everything is organized around two essential notions: that of a new undertaking, of an *invention;* and that of *harmony,* of certain calculations that are to be the means of achieving it. Now, these notions are only evoked, and are left carelessly obscure. The *Illuminations* do not share that determination to analyze thoroughly that characterizes *Une Saison en enfer.*

And yet if we now read, in *Jeunesse, III (Vingt ans): exiled, the voices of instruction,* and if we accept the idea that Rimbaud may have also referred, occasionally, to the failure of his undertaking, another poem, *Solde,* very close in spirit and style to those of this group, will perhaps enlighten us about what this *invention* was to entail. *For sale* (. . .), Rimbaud writes here, *the voices reinstated: a fraternal awakening of all choral and orchestral energies, and their immediate application; the occasion, the unique moment, to unchain our senses! (. . .) For sale—the uses of calculation, unknown harmonic intervals. Discoveries and unsuspected terms, immediately available.* The context is the out-of-business sale of all Rimbaud's hopes. This poem might authentically be a final poem, where a last reserve of credulity and energy is swallowed up by sarcasm. But for this very reason we see here shining for an instant, before night carries it away, what had been hoped for: *Bodies and voices for sale (. . .) For sale: priceless bodies, beyond race or world, or sex, or line of descent.* What should have been, could we not say, a new incarnation of the divine, what had been *left unsold*, what today's *damned love* and the *infernal probity of the masses*, devoted to Good and Evil, have always ignored.

Did Rimbaud then mean to indicate in these words, *voices, awakening*, a kind of symphonic fulfillment of man's nature, a rhythmic, coherent, danced unleashing of the virtualities contained within his essence, a final repairing of those "sweet bells" that Ophelia, a witness for her own anxious time, deplored were out of tune in Hamlet?

To persuade ourselves of this, to grasp completely these yet uncertain notions, to rejoin Rimbaud in the fullness of his new idea—and to find him therefore as rich as ever in energy and spirit of invention—we have only now to read the extraordinary poem *Génie*, one of the most beautiful in the French language, but one which would remain among the most obscure in any perspective but this. For this is not Christ, as some have tried to say, this creature of speed and glory of whom Rimbaud can write: *Pride more benevolent than charities lost.* On the contrary, his imperious action fulfills all the suggestions, all the ideas latent in the poems I have quoted. Thus *the occasion, the unique moment, to unchain our senses* is restated, reaffirmed, in *His body! Unchaining so long desired . . . ;* the invented *key* to love, a musical key, is reaffirmed in *love, perfect and rediscovered measure;* and the entire poem is in truth the vehement assertion, in unsuspected depth, of *voices reinstated* in the new harmony.

Génie is an act of revolutionizing intuition, that cloudless moment of vision when a train of thought finds fulfillment.

With the blissful, discontinuous ardor of ecstasy, *Génie* evokes in his swift passage, at the very moment when he allows himself to be perceived—when he might also disappear—when he truly exists, a being who knows limits no longer, nor infirmity of space or time, because he is simultaneously *present* and *future* and infinity as he *goes on his way* through real space; a being who is *eternity*—as long as the word no longer designates the distant quality, the ever inaccessible condition of ever revocable gods, but a completely immanent faculty, anyone invested with it being able to actualize in the same instant all his potential and thus escape from the alienations of his body; a being, therefore, whose past vanishes at each instant in immediate freedom and possession; a being who, beyond his old identity as *I*—which today is stifled by the crushing weight of being *someone else*—retrieves sovereign happiness as a kind of absolute *He*. A being, therefore, far beyond the present condition of man—but one whom we would be wrong to consider some sort of god. For if it is true that he reconsecrates the world by tearing it away from darkness and returning it to desire, he *who purified all that we drink and eat,* he who *has opened our house to winter's foam, and to the sounds of summer,* this is probably nothing else than the highest act that our humanity is capable of; and if it is true that he shines forth *in the storm-filled sky and in banners of ecstasy,* above our horizon, let us understand that it is not at the limits of the natural world but metaphorically at those of existence: in the only space that has remained free and pure in our senseless condition, in that very sky filled with *illuminations* where the hope of the young Rimbaud once took shape. The *génie* is here, Rimbaud infers it when he says that we have only to recognize him and follow him. And if, like a god, he makes us a *promise*, it is merely the promise of human possibility—*O delight of our well-being, brilliance of our faculties, selfish affection and passion for him*—when, its moral fetters finally broken, it can return to the *infinity* of the glorious virtualities that we perceive in our strength, our intelligence, and our senses.

I think of Michelangelo's *Slaves,* imprisoned in matter, but imprisoned above all in psychological fatality, paralyzed by the mysterious weakness of an ego that dares no longer actuate its desire. Rimbaud's *génie* is not a god who turns his face toward men. He is man absolute, freed, carrying to their conclusion within his own essence *vaster migrations than the old invasions were,* these latter being, after all, no more than one of the forever blind and awkward attempts of historical man to recover *the true life.* He is a man, in short, who has passed from abstention to action, from alienation to presence, from law to freedom, and consequently from penury to the tragic, from the penury of an exile from the world to the tragic at the heart of being, which Rimbaud conveys to us in these few boundless words: *O World! and the shining hymn of new sorrows . . .*

He has evoked in *Génie* what I may call our virtuality of glory; and, as in *Soleil et chair,* in fact, as in his first "naive" poems, he has once more decided to attach himself to man's essence and his powers, rather than to his factual condition and his disheartening weaknesses.

III

We must now devote ourselves resolutely to this new perspective, make clear the contrast between *Génie* and *Une Saison en enfer,* between *pride* and *charity,* and finally between two conceptions of love, if we wish to find the key to this enigmatic undertaking.

When Rimbaud writes, in *Génie* again: *He is love, perfect and rediscovered measure; reason, marvelous and unforeseen; he is eternity: the beloved prime mover of the elements, of destinies,* is it possible to equate this generous *reason* with the *glowing patience* proposed at the end of *Une Saison en enfer?*

But in the *Saison* Rimbaud never spoke of a love so profoundly in accord with man's virtualities of glory. There he defined charity, love of people and things for what they are, and such as they are, in the *gnarled reality* of earth, far from *supernatural powers,* from the *feasts* and *triumphs* he explicitly condemned. And such a concept, if not completely Christian, was at least decisively determined by the words of Christ.

Completely different are the latent metaphysics, the background of *Génie.* For *reason, measure,* and the *beloved prime mover* as they appear in this poem evoke a well-defined image of the world. This is the cosmos of Greek thought, where the Good appears identical with measure, the soul of the world identical with the rigorous and eternal machinery of the heavens, and love identical with the discovery, deep within the realm of the senses, of the infinite harmony of numbers and of universal reason. We do not force the meaning of this last word in the *Illuminations* if we see it in a summons to a good which is order, reality, and beauty indiscernably. In a poem quite close to *Génie*, dedicated *A une raison* (To a reason), it says: *Your finger strikes the drum, dispersing all its sounds, and a new harmony begins,* which clearly suggests that this reason opposes its power of organization to the confused data of the senses. Is not the love spoken of in *Génie*—"l'amor che muove il sole e l'altre stelle—" the prime mover of the sun and the planets, which themselves in their ordered movement are the supreme reason of all things, even of our faculties and our destinies? As Rimbaud says: the *beloved prime mover of the elements, of destinies?*

In such a conception, in any case, law is no longer the moral obligation, the child of Good and Evil, from which Rimbaud has suffered so much. It is the reflection of order, it is also consonance, it is our participation in the intelligible essence of being (we know that the same word in Greek, *nomos*, denoted the common chord in both society and music), and I have done no more, in thus examining the background of *Génie*, than to expose its clearly manifest rejection of the *ancient genuflections*, of the Christian universe of sin. And yet an ambiguity remains. All is not "Greek" in this poem which deals with a decision, a commitment, a future; and all that is Greek is not to be found in it. We do not find in its impatient ardor the recommendations of detachment of a philosophy whose every school concludes with words of wisdom. If *Génie* contains the mutation of an obscure condition into freedom and glory, it is not accomplished by contemplation but by action, as if a wind has forced the motionless perfection of the empyrean into the ongoing movement of existence. And if we have to let *Génie* remain in a Hellenic perspective, it might perhaps be better to compare it first of all to Pythagorean or Orphic concepts, that is, to religious speculations founded on Mysteries and on the idea of salvation. It is for man and for man alone, *Génie* says, that reason and nature exist. Our deepest concern is not with the ordered heavens. The truth is that Rimbaud has been too much involved in the existential thinking of Christianity to forget its categories. And in order to understand his ambition, we must place it within an incredibly dynamic synthesis of the Greek cosmos and of the Alexandrian anthropocentric dreams of salvation, closer to a

Christ lord of the world than to the Plotinian procession of the hypostases.

At any rate, we can now, and must now, as a basis for this small group of poems, assert the idea of a natural harmony where sin no longer exists, nor consequently that *other love*, the suffering selfless love of charity. From this point on the step from the human to the divine is no more than the step from the virtual to the actual. There is no more need for a history of the soul, for error in the past or redemption in the future, for a God who will or will not deign to come down from His heaven; it is in the profundity of the instant that man will rediscover his immanent divinity: *He will not go away, nor will he come down again from some heaven. He will not fulfill the redemption of women's fury nor the gaiety of men, nor the rest of this sin; for he is, and is loved . . . and so it is already done. Unchaining so long desired,* the *terrible speed in acts and forms* depends only on *a more intense music,* and now Rimbaud's allusions to *a fraternal awakening of all choral and orchestral energies,* to the musical key to love, become clear. Man, like all creation, is potential music. It is up to him, to him alone, through the elaboration of a practical gnosis, to reawaken his almost silent voices. Obviously, the Rimbaud who wrote *Génie* is no longer the *Visionary,* either. Reality in his eyes remains a rhythm, but this new Rimbaud no longer believes that the poet needs to be the *horrible worker* who exhausts himself and *croaks* in the ecstatic revelation of the unknown. Rhythm and the future are within us like some attainable perfection and it is no longer violence but a *key* that will let us set them free.

IV

Thus, if the descriptions I have tried to offer of Rimbaud's ideas between the *Lettre du voyant* and the completion of *Une Saison en enfer* are the least bit accurate, neither the excruciating ecstasy of his first stay in Paris nor the salvation he later sought in charity has anything to do with this absolute exercise in life that the poems grouped around *Génie* and *Jeunesse* identify with the awakening of a profound harmony. Here, from *Génie* to *Solde*, from hope to failure, we find a plan unlike any other, and a precise event, which we must now situate in Rimbaud's development if we wish to understand all the aspects of his poetry. The problem is difficult, because we cannot simply rely on differing conceptions to infer that they appeared at different periods. A writer may quite easily yield to two opposed intuitions during the same period of time, projecting even before the intuited failure of one the intellectual foundations of the other, and consequently he may make side by side two simultaneous experiments in form, write certain passages of the *Illuminations* at the same time as *Une Saison en enfer*. There is in the poetic understanding, even if it is engaged as clearly as Rimbaud's in self-testing and thus in change, a simultaneity of inclinations that we must never forget, for it is the very measure of its concern for reality. Even moments of violent affirmation like *Génie* may dominate the consciousness for only a very brief moment, and have only interrupted for a while the evolution I have previously described of Rimbaud's plan of *selfless love*.

Yet, besides the fixed point of *Vingt ans*, which still proposes—so great is the cohesion of the poems I have cited—that we assign them all to the fall of 1874; and besides—from the more dialectical and fast-moving *Saison en enfer* to these polyphonic poems—an appearance of greater maturity in the means of expression, there is also the fact that certain of the *Illuminations* seem able, in light of the concepts of *Génie* now perhaps clearer, to make apparent an evolution beyond the pages of *Adieu*.

First of all, *Après le déluge*. This poem is the first recopied in the largest of the manuscript fragments we have, and I am astonished that no one has ever really paid attention to the rejection it contains of a past that can only be *Une Saison en enfer*. And yet how simple it is, when we consider it in this light! *After the Flood* (after the coming, but also after the end, of the desire for destruction) life has begun again, it's true, *the beavers were building, caravans departed,* the joyful news of spring's arrival is heard, but from the very first words this seeming joy strikes us with unexpected reservations. *As soon as the thought of the Flood had subsided, a hare stopped in the clover and trembling bell-flowers, and said his prayers to the rainbow, through a spider's web.* This is surely the only sentimental line the mature Rimbaud ever wrote; like all sentimentality it hides a lie, and the lie is soon recognized: *Oh! what precious stones were hiding, what flowers were already looking down. . . .* For a flower, *to look down,* as is shown in the poem's last paragraph, means to open and wither. Reality, brilliant and pure for an instant, darkens almost immediately. It returns to its usual state *(the sea, up there)* of undiminished frustration, where the child *in the great house, its window panes still streaming,* must once more seek in *marvelous picture books* the precarious help of illusion. So Rimbaud brusquely reveals his new impatience: *Rise, pond—Foam, roll over the bridge and through and over the woods; black hangings and organ music, lightning and thunder—rise up in torrents; waters and sadness, rise and raise up the Floods!* What, finally, are these floods, consequences of *sadness,* if not the spirit of negation and revolt, the violent denial of all human order that is announced in the *Lettre du voyant* and evoked again in the prologue to *Une Saison en enfer? I have called for plagues,* cries Rimbaud in the latter text. He says also that he has left his treasure in the care of *witches,* and these we find once more loved and solicited in the final lines of this first *Illumination.*

It is not the *rainbow* of a new alliance with being, it is *boredom* that has followed this end of the flood that Rimbaud had hoped to bring on by writing *Une Saison en enfer.* And I think that *Après le déluge* contains a remembrance of the autumn months of 1873 whose sadness is so evident in Garnier's portrait.[2] Rimbaud has quickly lost the *glowing patience* he had hoped for. He remembers now that he had once depended upon refusal and pride for his mysterious ability to question appearances, and he is ready once more to go back to *the Queen, the Witch who lights her fire in an earthen pot*—to all the drugs of illusion.

2. The date painted on the face of Garnier's painting (1873) is obviously more conclusive than the date written by hand on the back (1872). It seems certain to me that the portrait was done in the fall of 1873 when Rimbaud came back to live in Paris for the first time since June 1872, perhaps once more on rue Campagne-Première.

He is prepared as well for any new encounter, any adventure of the mind, as is shown in *Conte*, where the Prince, unable in spite of his violence to destroy anything, met a *Génie* who made him an enigmatic promise and disappeared with him into *essential health.*

I have already said that nothing remains of Rimbaud's life between October 1873 and spring of the following year. Whatever *classical sciences*, whatever *unimagined luxury* he experienced, we are no longer able to know.

But one poem in the *Illuminations* relates a staggering discovery, and perhaps now is the moment to examine it, so close does it appear to the *essential health* mentioned in *Conte* as well as in *Génie*. Between *Matinée d'ivresse* and *Génie* in particular the links are numerous. Here once again is the *unheard-of work*, the *marvelous body*. The promise of *Génie (Away with these ages and superstitions, these couplings and these bodies of old!)* corresponds to *that superhuman promise made to our souls and our bodies created again; that promise, that madness! Elegance, science, violence! They promised to bury in shadows the tree of good and evil, to banish tyrannical honesties, so that we might flourish in our very pure love.* This is the same idea of a future beyond Christian morality, full of strength and glory. But unlike *Génie*, which is devoted to the description in absolute terms of what will, or might, be the possible profundity of life, *Matinée d'ivresse* is a poem of inauguration, the account of the event in which the promise was made manifest. *Little drunken vigil, blessed!* It is *for the first time*, after *all this boorishness*, that the body appears *marvelous*, and that a *method* is revealed. And several aspects of the inaugural event, without being really stated, are easily discernible in the feverish writing that seems here to grasp the moment. On one hand the *fanfare;* if not real music, at least the affinity of the mysterious act with music. *Hideous fanfare where yet I do not stumble!* writes Rimbaud. We think of the *moving and sonorous suffering* that *dissolves in more intense music,* in *Génie,* and of all the allusions to music that *Solde* or *Guerre* or *Jeunesse* have associated with *the occasion, the unique moment, to unchain our senses*—with the new health.

And on the other hand, *poison. We believe in poison,* adds Rimbaud. He also says: *This poison will stay in our veins even when, as the fanfare departs, we return to our former disharmony.* And finally: *For this is the Assassins' hour.* This time there is no ambiguity, and a secret is revealed.

For—I am not the first to have thought it[3]—these assassins are surely no other than the Hashishins, who also gave their *lives completely, every day,* because they had sworn allegiance to the Old Man of the Mountain, who dispensed the faithful from observation of the Law. Why is it so astonishing that Rimbaud should have known the etymology proposed by Sylvestre de Sacy? He had merely to read *Les Paradis artificiels (Le Poème du haschisch,* Chapter II), and we know that he did. Further, once we make the hypothesis of the drug, the whole poem becomes clear. *It began with a certain disgust,* writes Rimbaud, and Baudelaire describing the effects of hashish speaks of "a kind of repulsion and feelings of nausea." *It began with the laughter of children,* notes Rimbaud, and Baudelaire speaks of an incomprehensible hilarity, "a first phase of childish gaiety," in his own words. He alludes further to a "feeling of coldness in the extremities" and this probably explains *the angels of fire and ice* in *Matinée d'ivresse,* as well as the numerous evocations of cold or of freezing *(And the dream grows cold . . .)* in several *Illuminations.* Another proof, indeed, of a use of hashish is that it reappears in several poems. It is not necessary to have the key to the word *assassin* to want to group around *Matinée d'ivresse* a whole ensemble of texts which seem either to define or to describe the fantasies of the smoker or eater of hashish. *H,* for example, whose parallelism with *Matinée d'ivresse* can be demonstrated word for word. Then, without trying to be exhaustive, *Nocturne vulgaire, Being Beauteous, Angoisse, Antique, Barbare,* fluid, impressionistic narratives where the habitual elements of fantasy, a transfigured hearth, for example, are easily discernible. *One breath (. . .) dispels the limits of the hearth (Nocturne vulgaire). At the back of the black hearth, real suns on seashores (Veillées). Bright fires, raining in squalls of sleet—Delight! Fires in the rain*

3. Cf. Maurice Saillet, *Sur la route de Narcisse* (Paris, 1958), pp. 127 seq.

of a diamond wind thrown from this terrestrial core, charred forever, and for us. O World! (Far from old retreats and ancient flames we hear and feel). In this last poem, *Barbare*, we find Rimbaud, *long after days and seasons pass, and the living have gone, and the countries*, as if shut up in that *magnificent house*, in the *illustrious retirement*, where he learns to extract a world from his solitude *(O Delight, O world, O music!)*, thanks to the ancient poison.

The *poison* of *Matinée d'ivresse* is assuredly hashish. And everything from now on comes down to an essential question: In what way can hashish associate itself with music, to constitute the *method* all these poems speak of, supposing—or, in my opinion, taking for granted—that these hashish-inspired *Illuminations* are too closely related to *Génie*, to *Solde*, to *Jeunesse*, too clearly the consequence of the boredom of *Après le déluge*, not to have been written during the months that followed *Une Saison en enfer?*

V

Of course, it is necessary to recall here that the drug experience is rather an old one for Rimbaud. In his *Souvenirs familiers*, Ernest Delahaye assures us that his friend had taken hashish as early as the fall of 1871, in the very first months of his stay in Paris; but he had seen nothing but black and white moons, and he even spoke bluntly of this *artificial paradise* as a *perfect flop*. The landscapes of hashish have no place in the poems of 1872, and it is evident that if drugs were used then in any methodical way, they were merely one of the means of the *systematized disorganization* and only aimed at destroying the realm of appearance, without particular abandon to any one of their mirages. The function and importance of hashish or opium in England during the months spent there with Verlaine is less clear. There is no doubt that the experiences of Paris were continued and even expanded. In Isabelle's description Rimbaud, when he came back to Roche in May 1873, showed all the signs of the most severe intoxication, and it has often been concluded that the enthusiasm expressed in *Matinée d'ivresse* refers to this period. Yet, although Rimbaud wrote in *Vagabonds: I was creating, beyond a country haunted with bands of rare music, the ghosts of future nocturnal luxury*, he adds immediately: *After this vaguely hygienic distraction . . .* Nothing here yet resembles the brilliant and triumphant tone of the *little drunken vigil*.

I imagine that for a long time Rimbaud did not particularly care for hashish. His ingrained realism must have detested the illusions that drugs induce, and *Nuit de l'enfer* in fact denounces their falsehoods rigorously: *Ah stop! . . . enough of those errors someone whispers to me —magic spells, deceptive odors, childish music.* In *Barbare* Rimbaud will still say: *Oh! A banner of raw meat that bleeds on the silk of seas and arctic flowers; (they do not exist).* Of what use is a moment's paradise to someone who wants to establish *the true life*, to rediscover the state of *child of the sun?* Honesty and hope teach us to prefer the hell of unquenchable desire, even if an evil genius suggests that its fire is *despicable* and its anger is *horrible and silly. Dear Satan* wants to torment us even more with his balms followed by terrible awakenings.

But the happiness of drugs has two aspects, and is able to seduce even the mind most hostile to vain images.

What strikes us most in *Matinée d'ivresse* is an absence of reference to any transfigurations of the outside world. *Oh, that will be* my *Beautiful,* my *Good!* writes Rimbaud. He underlined the two possessives, making emphatically clear in the very first words of the poem that the experience above all has to do with him. He speaks of *the marvelous body, for the first time,* of a *superhuman promise made to our souls and our bodies created again,* he alludes to former boorishness, and everything thus confirms that this time the hashish acted specifically on the suffering and anxious *I.* Rimbaud suddenly saw himself in another light. And although he does not forget that it will soon pass, that *as the fanfare departs, we return to our former disharmony,* he does not seem to regard as an illusion what he now feels. Indeed, I believe that Rimbaud's attitude to drugs changed to the exact extent that his philosophy had changed. As long as he sought the true life in the disordering of sensorial data, hashish could offer him nothing. But when he came to think that the human individual is a nexus of powers and glorious possibilities, a virtual excellence, he was prone to seek in the trance of intoxication an occasion to perceive with his own eyes, within his own revealed body, the perfection to come. If human reality is a promise tarnished by the lethal sleep of this debased existence, why should not drugs, which weaken our everyday eyes, lead to its true subjectivity our consciousness unfettered at last?

The hashishin—the "God-Man," as Baudelaire had called him—thus perceives and experiences his *génie*. If he cannot *immediately seize upon this eternity*, he has still the right to interpret it as the most truthful kind of revelation, and to try to actuate it by all the means that help to decipher and to bring about a possible harmony. And here, most naturally, we come back to music. In music also resides *the reason, marvelous and unforeseen* that moves the souls of planets and of men. If only hashish gives us an understanding of it (and the virtue of hashish, it would seem, is to increase to infinity the rapidity of sensual perception, the richness of intuition) music can become the *fraternal awakening of all choral and orchestral energies* evoked in *Solde, the occasion, the unique moment, to unchain our senses*, the new beginning of love.

Music has always played an essential role in philosophies or mysticisms of numbers. Harmony, Plato tells us in the *Timaeus*, is the soul's ally when it seeks to bring back order and unison to the periodic movements that have become disordered within us. We know the even more fruitful and dynamic link made between intoxication and music by Pythagorism and Orphism. The aim here is by means of music to discover the divine being that dwells within us—and thereby to alter our destiny. We remember moreover that Théophile Gautier, in *Le Club des Haschischins*, testified to the importance of music in the experiments carried out by his friends. My hypothesis is that Rimbaud as well wanted to associate drugs and music during hours of attentive study in order to awaken the powers of his mind. The *voices reinstated*, the *seance of rhythms*, the *unknown harmonic intervals, harmonic ecstasy*, are simply allusions to this *task*, one as concrete and rigorous as possible: to ask of musical chords, through the lucidity of hashish, to reveal our essence to us, by substituting for the psychological and moral causality that keeps us shut up in the universe of guilt, a rhythmic structure that will return us for a moment to the life of the cosmos.

And to make completely explicit Rimbaud's last plan, I turn now to one of the most important, but also one of the least understood of his poems, *Mouvement*, which is entirely of a piece (does it not speak of *harmonic ecstasy* and *the old brutishness?*) with the *Illuminations* I have so far considered.

MOUVEMENT

A winding movement on the slope beside the rapids of the river.
The abyss at the stern,
The swiftness of the incline,
The overwhelming passage of the tide,
With extraordinary lights and chemical wonders
Lead on the travellers
Through the windspouts of the valley
And the whirlpool.

These are the conquerors of the world,
Seeking their personal chemical fortune;
Sport and comfort accompany them;
They bring education for races, for classes, for animals
Within this vessel, rest and vertigo
In diluvian light,
In terrible evenings of study.

For in this conversation in the midst of machines,
Of blood, of flowers, of fire, of jewels,
In busy calculations on this fugitive deck,
Is their stock of studies visible
—Rolling like a dike beyond
The hydraulic propulsive road,
Monstrous, endlessly lighting its way—

Themselves driven into harmonic ecstasy
And the heroism of discovery.

Amid the most amazing atmospheric accidents,
Two youths stand out alone upon the ark
—Is it the old brutishness being pardoned?—
And sing, at their watch.

The *rapids*, the *overwhelming passage of the tide*, the *hydraulic propulsive road* have one obvious meaning: matter here reveals its virtual energy, the immense power whose mutation will be effected in *terrible evenings of study* by these *conquerors of the world*, the mathematicians and physicists. *Rest and vertigo*, the exact formulation and infinite practical application (the *uses of calculation* in *Solde*): science will actualize the numbers latent in nature. It will be the *vessel* that carries man's destiny, the new *ark* of a renewed future. Certainly Rimbaud, though he found science *too slow*, was always fascinated by its limitless capacity for reorganizing the facts of nature and of society.

But science, in the usual meaning of the term, will not explain the last four lines. And we will better understand these *two youths* if we compare them to other couples Rimbaud has evoked under the sign of revelation and ecstasy: the couple in *Royauté* or the one in *Conte*, the couple of the Prince and his Genie, of the man and his beloved, of course, but foreshadowed now, made possible by the meeting of the anxious mind with its potential for glory, far from the former *boorishness*. On board the last boat of Rimbaud's imagination there reappears the person, the individual self, who wants to metamorphose not only the material universe but also the subjective dimension or man's relation with himself. The truth is that Rimbaud did not conceive an opposition between the progress of science and his musical speculation. The same reason governing the visible universe and the realm of life, it is natural that the two undertakings·reveal themselves to be related, and both of them liberating energy, *wonder* and light, it is logical that one be the metaphor of the other and agree to give it a place in its *extraordinary* progression. It is even from their connection, from it alone, that it was possible to build this second ark, the one that will save not merely the physical life of man, but his threatened virtualities. But if science is a collective invention, subject to time, the transmutation of humanity remains an individual affair and can perhaps anticipate the transformation of nature. On the bridge of the ark, the new poet will keep apart, sing, and take up his watch, so that other men at least may see him and understand that a new epoch is at hand.

And it is surely one of the aspects of Rimbaud's harmonic plan to make heard a promise, and perhaps as well to begin the diffusion in society of the new spirit of glory. *Take one step,* he says to the *reason* that inaugurated a *new harmony,* and it will be *the rise of new men and their setting out. It is the role of force and justice,* as he says also in *Jeunesse,* to reverberate in *this dancing, this voice,* and to wage in their name, against *heredity and race* (that is, against the psychological and moral estrangement received from our Christian ancestors), the first absolute war announced in *Guerre: a war, of justice or force, of a logic beyond all imagining.* The social reflection begun in *Le Forgeron,* matured by the setbacks of the Commune, interrupted, but surely without being truly forgotten, in *Une Saison en enfer,* finds here a metaphysical conclusion that, at last, specifically expresses the imperatives and knowledge of the poetic experience.

VI

Will the reader now imagine I have described a Rimbaud who tried to change the nature of man by inventing chords on the keyboard of some instrument? That would confuse the idea with its practical realization; the early days of a plan with a labor that was probably never really undertaken.

"Hashish makes us like God" wrote Gérard de Nerval in *Le Voyage en Orient (A Journey to the East).* "Intoxication disturbs the eyes of the body, but opens wide those of the soul; the mind, freed from its heavy gaoler the body, takes flight like a prisoner whose guard has fallen asleep and left the key in the lock. It wanders joyous and free in space and light, talking familiarly with genies it meets, who dazzle it with sudden and charming revelations. Upon an easy wing it traverses atmospheres of indescribable happiness, and all within the space of a minute that seems an eternity, so swiftly does one sensation succeed another." Here are some impressions that Rimbaud has transposed in *Génie,* and even a few of his words; but also an indication of the true nature, illusory and short lived, of the spiritual ambition of the hashishin. The eater of hashish only dreams his thoughts. And Rimbaud's honesty, never long deceived, could not help but find this out.

The *Illuminations* are clearly, in any case, the recognition of a failure. Side by side with poems of happiness like *Matinée d'ivresse* or *Génie* are others that, while they remain under the sign of the harmonic undertaking, let doubts appear and at last even announce the bankruptcy of all hope. *Could She,* writes Rimbaud in *Angoisse, make me forgive the constantly defeated ambitions—will an easy final season repair ages of misery—will a day of success make us forget the shame of our fatal clumsiness?* He fears that *the Vampire who makes us kind* seeks only to amuse herself at the expense of those she entices. Similarly in *Royauté,* although there had been *revelation, and the end of tribulations,* and the mutual recognition of man and woman in the light of a brighter day, we still feel that evening will dissipate what was only an instant. And finally *Solde* is the renunciation I have already spoken of. We can understand the poem easily now, as the sale, at low prices, of impossible ambitions. The idea itself had been perhaps a good one, and there might be, thanks to *discoveries and unexpected terms,* a possibility of the *immediate possession* of our glorious virtuality. But this grasp is denied to our sleeping intelligence. As it says in *Conte,* as an everlasting conclusion: *Our desire lacks the music of the mind.*

Rimbaud may have recognized, in his reverie about music, with some chagrin, that *drunken sleep, stretched out on some strip of shore* he had been able to foresee, for the eve of some African departure, in *Une Saison en enfer;* and, in his final poems, those *few belated cowardices* he had also foretold.

A sign, in any case, of his renunciation of *the music of mind* is the return, in several poems, of an obsession with reality as thingness, events irremediably worn out, the reality that from the age of twenty will circumscribe his life within the deadly confines of his destiny. On that Sunday in the fall of 1874 it is not only the *seance of rhythms* that occupies his thoughts, it is also *a visitation of memories* and he even says of the latter that they interrupt his *study* for a moment. Now—and this is the supreme admission—these memories all relate to the earliest years of his consciousness, the ones that so obviously decided his future.

Along rivers the little children sit, he writes—and he was one of them —*stifling their curses.* Here is what is real and irreparable: the mysterious possibility, which was within reach but lost in the childhood years. *Man of average constitution*—I quote once more those admirable lines that express so sadly Rimbaud's incessant question—*was the flesh not once a fruit, hanging in an orchard? O infant hours! Was the body not a treasure to be unsparing of? Loving—either Psyche's peril or her strength?* And also in the last section of *Jeunesse: You are playing still at the temptation of Anthony.* When he tries to recreate, under the influence of hashish, the powers of the cosmic *eros,* it is always the humbler kind of love of one human being for another that obsesses him. As once before at the end of *Le Bateau ivre,* what he really wants is a place in the world of *Europe,* the world of ordinary people, because that place would be assigned to him and made secure for him through love. And now at the age of twenty, this desire and this regret are all the more overwhelming. For now, with *physical ingenuousness staled in bitterness,* it is quite possible that the chance to reinvent love has disappeared forever with the naiveté of childhood. Rimbaud's genius, that energy, that haste, will have been above all, as I have already suggested, an attempt to reinvent a capacity to love before—and so terribly soon!— it was forever too late. And now that the moment arrives, his sense of truth binds him to it with bitterness and dictates *Solde,* where the commercial metaphor shows the degradation into inert, worn-out objects, odds and ends, of his initial ambitions. Was Rimbaud one day to become a trader in order to continue this metaphor, and thus in a way to continue expressing the truth? From now on, in any case, he can look with harsh understanding at the *metropolis considered modern,* perfectly anonymous, peopled with beings in his own image, nonexistent: *because everything here looks like this: dry-eyed Death, our diligent daughter and servant; a hopeless Love.* . . . There is nothing left for him but to resign himself, as he tries to do in *Ville,* to the dark place of exile.

Impossibility and Freedom

Rimbaud stopped writing when the end of childhood, more compelling than any intellectual decision, deprived him of the hope that he could *change life*.

Attempts have been made recently to show that some of the *Illuminations* were written after 1874, and while the arguments that have been advanced are not at all convincing, it is possibly true.[1] Yet what do two or three returns to poetic expression mean, except that it may happen that hope and habit do not end all at once?

I would rather seek the spirit of these new years in a text whose date is unquestionable, and which denies with terrible violence all the pretensions of poetry. In October 1875, after a year spent in Germany and Italy, Rimbaud wrote to his friend Delahaye. He told him he was about to study for the "bachot" in science, but also he spoke, worriedly, about military service since his deferment was up, and he then improvised, or recopied in the letter, a little poem called *Rêve ("Dream")*. And here, in a few broken lines, in a ludicrous travesty, this ultimate libretto for a *fabulous opera* gathers for a last time and distorts and dismisses all the elements of the metaphysical drama that sealed his fate.

1. See Appendix II.

"RÊVE"

Everyone's hungry in the barracks—
    That's right!
    Blasts, and bursts of wind!
A Genie: I am Gruyère!
Lefebvre: Give me air!
The Genie: I am Brie!
The soldiers cut upon their bread—
    That's life! Whee!
The Genie: I am Roquefort!
    —We will die of it!
    —I am Gruyère,
    And Brie. . . . etc.

WALTZ
We are a pair, Lefebvre and I, etc.

The barracks, the evil-smelling place once evoked in *Le Coeur volé*, is our life, forever darkness and absence. When the soldiers *cut upon their bread*, Rimbaud says this plainly: *That's life!* And in the air of this place of dismal patience and hunger, we still find the *blasts* and *bursts of wind* he had once long ago asked to transfigure reality, but today, as once before in *Un Coeur sous une soutane*, he is able to do no more than emphasize their sordid character. If, from this dislocated and dark reality, from this nauseous sacredness, looms up once again a *genie*, the one who had once *purified all that we drink and eat*, the luminous bearer of a promise, is now all the more denounced. The new genie exclaims: *I am Brie! . . . I am Roquefort! . . . I am Gruyère! . . .* Rimbaud asserts that nothing exists beyond the most suffocatingly anti-poetic reality, even if—*we will die of it*, say the soldiers—he has in this defiance to renounce his ambition forever.

Another sign that Rimbaud's renunciation is final this time is the intense study of languages, German, Italian, Russian, then Arabic, and still others, that he began at the end of 1874. We must remember that poetry is attained only by giving absolute value to one's native tongue; and consequently understand as a secret and active disclaimer of poetry the new study of language in its various forms. Besides, according to Verlaine and Delahaye, Rimbaud had greatly changed. *"L'Homme"* of earlier years had become another Homais.[2] In Verlaine's grating but intuitive poem "Malheureux, tous les dons!" we find a Rimbaud who has yielded completely to obscenity, to derision, to anger, to the fascination of nothingness. The hope that the author of *Une Saison en enfer* tried vainly to rid himself of has grown very much weaker since.

Now, it may be, of course, that it would never be totally erased from his heart; that this hope, disguised from itself, was the reason for the travels that Rimbaud undertook in 1875 from one end of Europe to the other, and as far as Java[3]; that it was the secret energy, later responsible for his greedy accumulation of money. In this sense, Harar may not have been so much a denial of Rimbaud's past life as a continuation of it: concretely, when he thought of getting married, of raising a son, to begin again with him and through him a life that would be at least lucid, if not completely happy; and in a symbolic sense, if we can say that the kilos of gold he carried in his belt preserve the memory of the metaphysical sun he once searched for in vain, and cast over his most sensible plans the glow of a residual irrationality:

> If I forget my pain,
> If I can get some gold,
> Should I live in the North,
> Or the wine-blessed South?

Were not physical disability and disease once desired as the key to a new idleness, abandoned to the care, at last, of someone maternal? Hope

2. Homais, one of Flaubert's characters, a narrow-minded and militant rationalist.

3. Rimbaud travelled by working here and there at different jobs. He once enlisted in the Dutch army, and so got to Indonesia. He then deserted, returned to Europe, then left for the Mediterranean, and gradually restricted himself to the shores of the Red Sea, before settling in Harar as the agent for a trading company at Aden.

can, in fact, be a disease, a high disease that destroys all the balanced patterns of existence, that maims fate and even the body. But on the other hand it can endure on and on, deprived of all substance, in desperate situations. After his leg had been amputated, when he was delirious and condemned in his hospital room in Marseilles, Rimbaud dictated a few incoherent phrases: *I am completely paralyzed, and so I am anxious to be on board early. Please tell me at what time I must be aboard* . . . It was the day before he died; these are the last words he left. And yet in them we find all the categories of the hope I have tried to describe: the mysterious *paralysis*, product of the theft of love; the boat so often imagined as the very symbol of *the true life;* and as a bridge between the two, unconquerable, the irrational "and so" of hope.

But it was on the same hospital bed, during the last months of his life, that he referred to his poems as *winecask rinsings.*[4] Hope may have remained within him, but all its undertakings, as soon as he recollects them, are immediately judged by the *atrocious scepticism* that one of the last poems of the *Illuminations* evoked. By 1875 what in Rimbaud was conscious had given up trying to *change life.* And for this reason I do not intend in this book to recount his years of wanderings and crushing labor. To want to change life is to engage universality, to bear witness, to seek a dialogue with the consciousness of one's time. But whoever gives up the attempt to remake life shuts himself up within his own fate and has the right to have his privacy respected. I find it somehow indecent that one should track down a man who has returned to a life of anonymity. Let us not read Rimbaud's letters to his family from Africa; let us not try to find out whether the man who once hoped to become the *thief of fire* wound up selling this or that.[5]

4. The rinsing water of a wine barrel was sometimes used by the poorest farmers as "wine."
5. See Appendix III.

II

Let us rather pause before his grave, in this place devoid of mirage that so many young people have desired to visit, in the Charleville cemetery. Here, beneath a stone marked simply with a date, in the immobility of death, matter and limitation are triumphant: this so habitual degradation of reality into thing against which Rimbaud had struggled so much. And he was not brought low in the sacred way, the joyful way indeed, he had once dreamed, when he wanted to be a *golden spark of this light, nature,* so that death would have come as simply the final fusion. For this is a grave for a petit-bourgeois, a peasant, cramped, miserly, conforming. It makes clear that a life has been robbed of life, that a man has had to exchange a future for a fate, the freedom of a child of the sun for the burdened condition of trader and laborer. And yet, sealing that destiny, it assembles its elements; the early Rimbaud, the *Génie* that the mature man, at the end of his inventiveness and his strength, had finally driven out for having abused him with an impossible promise, is here once more beside the man who went to the ends of the earth to forget him the better. And for many who come here it is even he, this violent, immoderate genie, who stands before them and speaks. He seems to make of this stone his paradoxical authority. He denies the idea of failure. Let us pause at this impression, irresistible. It contains perhaps the most serious lesson we may receive from the poetry of Arthur Rimbaud.

But let us remember that there are two ways of thinking, two ways for the human spirit to move ahead.

The first is to think of freedom as no more than a choice among the diverse possibilities that our factual condition offers us. Since we cannot like the idea of random choice, this way of thinking leads us to assign value to objective knowledge and consequently to rational thought. Freedom, Hegel teaches us, is the knowledge of necessity. Anathema will soon be declared against anyone who refuses to understand the requirements or the rights of this necessity; or who refuses to choose.

Rimbaud, from this point of view, was worthless. He was unable to choose between the possibilities that in practice were offered to him. Neither contented bourgeois, nor consistent reformer, he did not "know" necessity, he did not even acknowledge it. Yes, indeed, from this reasonable point of view his poetry is a rambling that we must not justify. Even revolutionaries, those who challenge a stage in the social condition of man, must leave him to his unreason. If they accept his criticism of the old morality, it is only a tactical acceptance; they do not really understand him. Were he still alive they would ask him to be content with the new law, and would be ready to condemn him if he did not agree.

But the other mode of being claims the name of freedom as well: when the mind, in order to distinguish the best, no longer limits itself to the possibilities which it is offered. It fixes its desire in the absolute, and reserves the right to accept or to reject the suggestions of reality, depending on whether or not they satisfy this inalienable desire. And if the latter appears decidedly "impossible," it will yet maintain this desire, for it prefers its own exigence to any relative satisfactions. Forced to bear its condition, it yet will never consent to applaud things as they are. And sometimes it will even have the heroism, as I said in the early pages of this book, to bring an accusation against them. In such a case it assumes all frustrations, all misfortunes, and even aggravates them, in order to provide an absolute testimony. Such action in its eyes is far from being absurd, it is on the contrary the honor of man. And perhaps it even thinks it will force an issue. For the attitude I am speaking of is neither despairing nor stoic, and is ready to believe that things as they are may be metamorphosed as easily by miracle as ameliorated by reason. Trying through a decisive challenge to reawaken being to its liberty, it hopes to transmute the relationship between consciousness and nature, whose perenniality is the postulate of objective thought. Is not, indeed, the Hegelian "absolute knowledge" another death, and the worst? And is not a new freedom, a practicable eternity, possible for an eye unblinking in its refusal to accept as "natural" and even habitable the idea of limitation and of death?

In trying to define this second way of thinking I have outlined, I think, the quest of Arthur Rimbaud. Now, in this light, who will consider him vanquished?

For him, in this world of good and evil, in this world of the Law where we are born and die, what was *the impossible* was love.

He had had the intuition of a participation in a *true life* that *is absent* today, in an active confidence that he called love and identified with faith. And he saw the rejection of that primordial life in an epoch, his own, when the idea of good and evil had legitimized only a part of the natural virtualities and imposed it at the expense of all the others. It was a fatal dissociation, Rimbaud thought. That part of life's possibilities that is selected—and is now the only future we have—resides within reality like an abstraction, like a fact accomplished in advance. Its moments and its doings have the immobility of death. And the other part of human possibility, even if condemned, appears beyond as a light. Thus our existence is frustrated to its very core. All the richness of the senses, almost given and yet impracticable, is *bitter* to us. All self-awareness, since it reveals to man his own impotence, forces him into self-disdain. Every heart, consequently, is *crippled.* All possibility of communion is destroyed, because others, like ourselves, are prisoners of their mutilated existence. And it is sexuality that leads to the most dramatic conflicts. For it remains the first intimation of a salutary existence, yet since its true object, which is a life and not a body, is lacking, it can never be more than a stifled virtuality, an imperfect or misdirected activity. What might have been the very rhythm of participation in reality, here, under interdiction, leads only to *vice,* as Rimbaud will say.

A *hell,* he says also; the only future under the law. But rather than trying to escape from it in forgetfulness, in working with the satisfactions that are after all left to us, he decided to assume all its misery in order to effect its transmutation. Once before, upon the horizon of law as today, did they not say that a *Son of Man* had done the same thing, offering humanity liberation through a *new love?* The teachings of that saviour have in turn become a constraining legality, and Christ is now the *thief of energies,* but his former act has remained worth pondering. Like Christ, the poet of the future must put an end to the soul's *season in hell* by saying no to the law.

And Rimbaud, a first time, thought he had succeeded: when, by disintegrating the world of appearances, he tried to become the *thief of fire.* It would have been a *vision* of the beating heart of nature, and the sudden liberation of the energies of the true subjectivity regained. It was the old *self,* dark and inert, that was to be torn apart for the growth of a new being. All the *disorganizations, all forms of love, of suffering, of madness* would have brutally cut out of the poet the evil that the moral law caused to exist within him. But this ambition, so new in poetry, brought Rimbaud to nothing but failure. He thought—occasionally— he had attained the immediacy of nature, but he was unable to share with mankind the immense power he could believe he had seized. And, animated as he was by movements of ecstasy, he was almost wrecked on the reefs of the law's immobility.

But then he came to think it is within its own framework, without destroying it, that the law could be transcended. It was too late, he thought, in the universe that law had created for us, to find again the paths of a Panic existence. The being we once were has become irrevocably an individual, defined by his moral essence, and so affected by interdictions and taboos that he has now no future but one narrowed and partially dead. Still, he does have the freedom to assume that condition as his very essence; to love it in others and in himself; and to make of this *charity* the new love that provides men with a reason for existing. Rimbaud at once undertook this revivification of the wounded soul; and we know what insurmountable obstacles he met with once again: in becoming the person who was virtual in him, he returned, in that dark and suffering *I* he had fled from, to all the psychological ills of the person, neuroses of timidity, of guilt, and of pride that had forbidden him communion in love. Must one continue in solitude to assert the value of love, or admit that charity is nothing but *the sister of death?* This is the ambiguous conclusion of *Une Saison en enfer.* A faith hard to hold, a charity incapable of affirming itself in real encounters, precisely like the virtual love that the *heartless* Rimbaud had always possessed deep within himself, vast, and at the same time paralysed.

Rimbaud did nothing—therefore—but hurl himself against the impossible, and nothing was solved, and no miracle took place. He did not even make a clear choice—a philosophic choice—between the suffering individual and the glorious man, between Christianity and the Kabala, for he condemned his dreams of triumphs and joy in *Une Saison en enfer* soon to take them up once again, and once again abandon them, in his last prose poems. He was like the *puddle* in the Ardennes, in the month of May, that in the midst of a life everywhere renewed remained *dark and cold.* He failed, it will be said, and it is true indeed for his private endeavors, I mean the possessions he dreamed of having and never had. His absolute hope, after a few moments of fallacious joy, brought him only a long twilight existence, and certainly much bitterness.

And yet, who would dare say that this hope, so senselessly maintained, will not in the long run win the case? What progress his intuitions have made, already, in minds and hearts! A link has been established between Rimbaud and the future. Thanks to his refusals, his life has been for us a kind of ark where our pride has survived. Still placed in the situation that this poet denounced—the crisis of life, product of the alienating forces of science and historical Christianity combined—contemporary man can learn from Rimbaud many things to help him in his struggle. The difference between object and presence, between existence and simple survival. The ruinous antagonism between love and a certain kind of respect for moral law. A faith in life which, slowly growing and first changing mental attitudes, will one day determine the education of a child, an education at last positive. The possibility of a reconciled man still remains. *The earth* still has *hillsides fertile in princes and artists,* even if *heredity and line of descent drives us to crime and to mourning.* And the child who will be born thus protected from good and evil, the son Rimbaud wanted to raise in spiritual harmony, will at last be able to face life, and to seek boldly what can be done with it. For this child will not be freed for all that from the metaphysical *impossible.* The struggle initiated by Rimbaud may deliver life from its ethical bonds, but it will be only to replace it in the light of its ontological limitations. It will have liberated it from its ages of indigence, but only to expose it to the *new afflictions* of the tragic, afflictions whose voice *sings* high and clear, afflictions that Nietzsche has even described as an ecstasy of joy.

Rimbaud's greatness is and will be that he said no to this bit of freedom that in his time and place he could have made his, in order to bear witness to the alienation of man, and to summon him from his moral contradictions toward a tragic confrontation with the absolute. It is this decision and his resolution in it that make his poetry the most liberating (and consequently one of the most beautiful) in the history of the French language. A grave, yes. The grave of unattained salvations, of humble joys destroyed, of a life forever set apart by its own exigencies from all equilibrium and from every happiness. But the Phoenix of freedom, who comes to life in the ashes of hope, beats his young wings here in the air.

Appendix I

To be convinced that Rimbaud had long been under the influence of *La Sorcière*, it is enough to compare the beginning of the introduction to the book ("woman contrives, she imagines; she gives birth to dreams and to divinities. At times she is a *Visionary,*") with the *Lettre du voyant.* Even the origin of *I is someone else* is perhaps to be found in *La Sorcière,* for Michelet writes: "Greece, like all cultures, had its *energumens,* disturbed minds, possessed by spirits . . . Ever since that time we have with us these poor, wandering melancholics who detest themselves, who have a horror of themselves. Imagine, in fact, what it must be like to feel oneself double, to believe in *someone else* residing within you, who comes and goes," etc. (*Livre Premier,* Ch. I). We may also compare the letter to Delahaye dated *Jumphe* with this passage from the *Epilogue:* "I used to get up at exactly six o'clock, as the cannon from the arsenal gave the signal for work to begin. Six to seven was an admirable moment for me. . . ." The whole of this *Epilogue* in fact recalls the last pages of *Une Saison en enfer* in its style, its beautiful tone of confident gravity, and its moving assurance in the new spirit, which it makes analogous with the morning. Michelet reinforced Rimbaud's passionate interest in the future. He taught him that certain beings (and, for example, in ancient France, the Witch) are able to exclude themselves from a world made unnatural by an evil moral and social order, to confine themselves to nature, now "demoniacal" because it can be attained only by rejecting contemporary values, and there to begin a resistance, to prepare a liberated future for a lowly humanity whose ambitions are yet unsure. Michelet also interested Rimbaud in science, and we can better understand the *philomath* who nearly succeeded the former *Visionary* if we remember that Michelet said of the Witch: "She contains within her the beginnings of industry, especially modern industry, which cures and recasts man." It would be extremely interesting to develop this parallel (extended to Edgar Quinet) especially along the lines of the quotations that are made—unfortunately without matching them very accurately with Rimbaud's ideas—by Margaret A. Clarke in *Rimbaud and Quinet* (Sidney, 1945).

Appendix II

It could concern, in any case, only a very few poems. Out of the whole of the *Illuminations* several groups already stand out. One contains *Génie, Guerre, Jeunesse, Solde,* and to these we must add *Vies, A une raison, Mouvement, Angoisse,* and probably *Conte,* since in one way or another they all evoke the search for the new harmony; another contains *Matinée d'ivresse, Being Beauteous, Veillées, Mystique, Nocturne vulgaire, Fleurs, Barbare, H, Fairy,* and probably *Dévotion,* for in these the experience of hashish seems constantly crucial, and nothing tends to suggest their separation. I have proposed an approximate date for these two groups, and an earlier one (the fall of 1873) for *Après le déluge.* What remains? First, obviously, a third major group: *Les Ponts, Ornières, Villes, I* and *Villes, II,* which are almost consecutive in the Lucien-Graux MS, and *Promontoire,* which survived separately. These poems share great similarities of style. The vision of the world they contain is always disturbed in the same way, and it may be opium that has created these vast panoramas of precise but successive impressions. Nothing, moreover, links them to the more fluid and elemental notations we find in *Matinée d'ivresse* or *Barbare.* It is easy to imagine that this group dates from the spring of 1873, when Rimbaud and Verlaine frequented the port of London. Was it by chance that *Vagabonds,* which deals with their life together, is inserted among these poems (although it must have been written, I think, at the time that Rimbaud copied them into the manuscript now known as the Lucien-Graux MS)? These, then, (and perhaps *Esplanade,* mentioned in a letter) may be the remains of an early effort on Rimbaud's part to carry out Baudelaire's program of "poetic prose," whose ideal, wrote the author of *Les Fleurs du mal,* derives from "familiarity with great cities." Of course, I do not forget that the poems called *Villes* have been compared to a certain page in Flaubert's *Tentation de saint Antoine,* which was not published until 1874. Did Rimbaud at that time rework some of his old poems, or complete some that had remained drafts? It is difficult, and would be rash, to decide.

It is equally difficult to date the few poems that remain: *Départ, Phrases, Ouvriers, Parade, Enfance,* and *Aube, Métropolitain, Soir historique, Ville, Bottom.* The first describes one of the archetypes of Rimbaud's thought, and might belong to any period. *Phrases* may be a selection made from older poems (dating from July 1872 in Belgium to the fall of 1873?). *Ouvriers* makes an allusion to a northern *February* which can scarcely be that of 1874, since

Rimbaud had only just gotten to London, and in the company of Germain Nouveau. Possibly the *Henrika* who is so closely associated with images of separation and impotence appeared in Rimbaud's life in February 1873 in London *(I have seen women's hell over there . . .)* and perhaps he recalls this when he returned the following year, at the time he was writing a poem with an analogous title, *Vagabonds. Parade* might be of the same reflective mood, and is associable in any case with one of Rimbaud's sojourns in England, like *Métropolitain* and *Bottom.* As for *Aube* and *Enfance,* I see principally their relation to *Après le déluge.* As for *Ville* and *Soir historique,* their relation, made of sadness and disappointment, to *Solde.* It is quite possible that all the *Illuminations* were written before the end of 1874.

Appendix III

It may be observed with some surprise that this portrait of Rimbaud does not take into account his deathbed conversion to Catholicism. Here are my feelings on the subject. Believers have certainly the right to consider as a certitude eventually reached by Rimbaud a change of mind that all agree was sudden, and that occurred in his exhaustion and delirium, but only if they are willing also to acknowledge their conviction as an act of faith. And as long as they do not attempt to reinterpret Rimbaud's past life in light of this supposed surrendering to God. It is not true, as some Catholic authors have been pleased to state, that Rimbaud's life was the flight of a conscience before a divinity it had tried to deny—up to the final moment when, vanquished and ravished, it yielded to that inexorable love. Such a conception has the virtue of turning this exemplary destiny into indirect evidence of the existence of God. But if one does not want to prove anything, is it not clear that it contradicts an entire body of poetry that was as lucid as it tried to be honest? The fact was that Rimbaud wanted to *change life.* And if God had been able to help him in this task by the mere fact of His existence, he would gladly have sold Him his soul. Several times—but always in vain—he did everything he could to believe in Him. *On my hospital bed, the odor of incense came so strongly back to me* . . . That "conversion" in Marseilles was surely not the first burst of Christian hope in this soul who was unable to forget the promise of Jesus. But all the other times—as long as Rimbaud retained consciousness—the fact is that God never answered. Often the Christian God was hated for the ethics he seemed to support, and sometimes waited for *gluttonously,* but in any case in *Une Saison en enfer* and the *Illuminations* He is always an absence, and if Rimbaud's work has any value as testimony, it is clearly and only as a witness to that *death* of the divine that Nietzsche also described. Find in this dying man's conversion the sign of God's awakening, those who wish, or can. But let us not seek His presence in poems that often called upon Him, but met with nothing but His silence.

Chronology

1854   20 October. Arthur Rimbaud is born in Charleville, Ardennes.

1860   Birth of his sister Isabelle.

1865   October. Rimbaud enters the Charleville *Collège*.

1869   He wins first prize in Latin poetry in the *Concours Académique* (with the poem *Jugurtha*); he writes *Les Etrennes des orphelins*.

1870   He studies rhetoric under Georges Izambard. On 24 May he writes to Théodore de Banville, and sends in addition to other poems *Credo in Unam*, later called *Soleil et chair*.

1870   29 August. First flight from home. Rimbaud was arrested on 31 August at the Gare du Nord. He was set free through the help of Georges Izambard, who brought him to stay with him in Douai, then sent him back to Charleville. Ten days later, a second flight, on foot, by way of Fumay, Charleroi, Brussels, to Douai. On the way he writes *La Maline*, *Au Cabaret vert*, *Ma Bohème*, etc. Sent back to his mother's under police escort.

1870   31 December. Mézières, a suburb of Charlevelle, is bombed and burnt.

1871   25 February. Third flight, by train, to Paris; Rimbaud stays there for about two weeks.

1871   15 May. Back in Charleville, he sends the "Voyant letter" to Paul Demeny.During the summer he writes to Paul Verlaine, and goes to Paris to meet him at the end of September. His main writings since May are *Le Bateau ivre* and *Ce qu'on dit au poète à propos de fleurs*. In Paris he spends time with Verlaine, Jean Richepin, Carjat, Cabaner, Forain, etc.

1872   Rimbaud spends the month of March in the Ardennes. He is in Paris again in May and June. during this spring he composes his most beautiful poems: *Mémoire*, *Age d'or*, *Bannières de mai*, *Michel et Christine*, etc. In July he leaves Paris with Verlaine to go to Belgium. The two friends reach London in September, but Rimbaud returns to Charleville just before Christmas.

1873   London again until April. Then to Roche, where he begins the composition of *Une Saison en enfer*.

1873   27 May. Rimbaud returns to London with Verlaine. The latter leaves for Brussels on 3 July, where Rimbaud joins him on the

7th. 10 July, Verlaine wounds Rimbaud with a revolver, and is sentenced to prison. Rimbaud returns to Roche, where he finishes writing *Une Saison en enfer*, which is published by Poot and Co. in Brussels. Rimbaud moves to Paris in the fall.

1874   Rimbaud goes to London in the spring with the poet Germain Nouveau. He stays there most of the year; the greatest part of the *Illuminations* are most probably written there.

1875   Working as a tutor in Stuttgart in January. Verlaine goes to see him at the beginning of March. In May he goes to Italy on foot. Spends time in Milan. Back in Charleville in the fall, Rimbaud continues studying languages (Spanish, Arabic, Italian, etc.)

1876   Rimbaud enlists in the Dutch Colonial Army, is sent to Batavia, deserts and returns to France.

1878–1879   Rimbaud is in Cyprus, as a building foreman near Larnaca.

1880   Another trip to Cyprus. Later he looks for a job "in every port on the Red Sea coast." In Aden, in November, a contract with Vianndy et Bardey. He arrives at the trading post in Harar on 13 December.

1881–1890   Trading and exploration in Harar.

1886   The *Illuminations* (I-XXXVII) are published in *La Vogue*, undoubtedly without Rimbaud's knowledge.

1891   8 June. Rimbaud returns from Africa and is admitted to Conception Hospital in Marseilles. His right leg is amputated. From the end of July until 23 August, a last visit to the Ardennes.

1891   10 November. Rimbaud dies in Marseilles, in Conception Hospital.

73 74 75 76 77 10 9 8 7 6 5 4 3 2 1